Reaching and Teaching Children Who Hurt

Reaching and Teaching Children Who Hurt

Strategies for Your Classroom

by

Susan E. Craig, Ph.D.
AGH Associates, Inc.
Hampton, New Hampshire

·P·A·U·L·H·
BROOKES
PUBLISHING CO.®

Baltimore • London • Sydney

Paul H. Brookes Publishing Co.
Post Office Box 10624
Baltimore, Maryland 21285-0624
USA

www.brookespublishing.com

Manufactured in the United States of America by
Versa Press, Inc., East Peoria, Illinois.

The information provided in this book is in no way meant to substitute for a
mental health practitioner's advice or expert opinion. Readers should consult a
mental health professional if they are interested in more information. This book is
sold without warranties of any kind, express or implied, and the publisher and
authors disclaim any liability, loss, or damage caused by the contents of this book.

The examples in this book are composites. Any similarity to actual individuals or
circumstances is coincidental, and no implications should be inferred.

Library of Congress Cataloging-in-Publication Data

Craig, Susan E.
  Reaching and teaching children who hurt: strategies for your classroom / by
  Susan E. Craig.
    p.   cm.
  Includes bibliographical references and index.
  ISBN-13: 978-1-55766-974-2 (pbk.)
  ISBN-10: 1-55766-974-0 (pbk.)
    1. Problem children—Education—United States.   2. Children with social dis-
abilities—Education—United States.   I. Title.

LC4802.C73 2008
371.930973—dc22   2008019916

British Library Cataloguing in Publication data are available from the British
Library.

2017

10   9   8   7

Contents

About the Author

Susan E. Craig, Ph.D., has devoted her professional career to teaching both children and adults. Her interest in the relationship between family violence and learning began early. While working as a young reading specialist, she noted that many of the children she evaluated had a history of family violence. Her interest piqued, she pursued a doctorate at the University of New Hampshire, studying under Murray Straus, Ph.D., world renowned for his research on family violence. Dr. Craig's 1986 dissertation established a relationship between children's exposure to violence and subsequent learning problems in language, memory, impulsivity, self-differentiation, and executive function. These findings, published in *Phi Delta Kappan* in 1992, are now confirmed by magnetic resonance imaging (MRI) technology, which documents the relationship between violence and brain development.

Dr. Craig completed a postdoctoral fellowship at the University of Miami. Working with Miami's Children's Protective Services and the assessment team at Jackson Memorial Hospital, she conducted intellectual evaluations of children who had been maltreated. During this time, she completed a 30-year retrospective study of child homicide in Dade County, Florida, which was published in the *Journal of Interpersonal Violence* in 1989.

Working on site with many school districts throughout the country, Dr. Craig supports teaching and administrative staff in creating inclusive, trauma-sensitive schools. In 2001, the Rockland County New York Bureau of Children's Educational Support (BOCES) received the National School Board Association Magna Award. The honor was in recognition of a program that Dr. Craig helped develop.

Foreword

The issue of trauma is not new to schools. Teachers are well aware of it and, perhaps without giving it a name, have been dealing with trauma's impact for generations. What is new is that we now know how pervasive the problem really is. The Centers for Disease Control and Prevention–funded Adverse Childhood Experiences (ACE; Felitti et al., 1998) study found that more children than we ever thought have experienced physical, sexual, and emotional abuse, have a mother who is treated violently, or have a household member with substance abuse or mental health issues. Simultaneously, the neurobiological field has been brimming with research explaining how these adverse experiences can influence a child's brain development. Toxic or overwhelming experiences can result in problems with language, executive functioning, attention, emotional and behavioral regulation, memory, and/or relationships. These difficulties can play out at school in seemingly intractable problems with learning, behaving, and forming relationships with adults and other children.

But, as we watch children walk into the school doors each day, we know that just as toxic experiences can have a negative impact, positive events can have a healing affect on a child's development. Every day we see children who have experienced the unspeakable go on to be successful. The problem comes when there are too many tragedies or too many children needing more than caring educators can provide. As Judith Herman (1992) explained in her classic book *Trauma and Recovery,* without a system of support, adults in caring positions can become overwhelmed and almost forced to turn away. Unfortunately, when educators don't know how to deal with trauma's impact or don't have the needed supports, they may resort to punitive approaches to address inappropriate or unexpected behaviors. This can retraumatize children and lead to negative educational outcomes.

Schools are communities for children, and it is important that they be safe havens for children who may live in homes that feel less than safe. If educators have an understanding of trauma's impact on learning, behavior, and relationships, and if they have a schoolwide system of support, they can help children to be successful despite any adversity they may have endured.

Susan Craig has provided us with strategies that are desperately needed in classrooms across the country to help traumatized children to be successful. Ms. Craig is a pioneer in this field, starting with her influential article, "The Educational Needs of Children Living in Violence," published in 1992, even before the recent wave of neurobiological research. *Reaching and Teaching Children Who Hurt: Strategies for Your Classroom* is a critical next step: providing strategies that educators can use directly in the classroom.

Teachers cannot take on the issue of trauma alone. Dealing successfully with childhood trauma necessitates the creation of environments within schools that are supportive for traumatized children, their parents, and the educators who teach them. A school context that is trauma sensitive is one that enables children to build caring relationships with adults and peers, self-regulate their emotions and behaviors, succeed in academic and nonacademic areas, and be physically and emotionally healthy (Massachusetts Advocates for Children, 2008).

Educators will make the best use of the rich information in *Reaching and Teaching Children Who Hurt: Strategies for Your Classroom* if trauma-sensitive classroom strategies are integrated into the overall climate and culture of the school. In order to support the use of these trauma-sensitive classroom approaches, several key elements should be in place, as detailed in *Helping Traumatized*

Children Learn: Supportive School Environments for Children Traumatized by Family Violence (Cole et al., 2005).

First, a trauma-sensitive school requires school leadership to play a key role. The senior administrator should help staff identify ways to integrate trauma-sensitive approaches into daily routines. Among other things, principals and headmasters must ensure there is time during the day for educators to meet in groups to brainstorm how to use the strategies in this book, both as part of an overall school policy and to focus on helping particular children who are especially needy.

Second, strong linkages between schools and mental health providers that go beyond individual counseling with students must be in place. Trauma-informed mental health providers can consult with and provide clinical supports directly to teachers, participate in consultations about individual children, do testing and evaluations, and give trainings and presentations. This, of course, requires mental health providers to understand the classroom strategies in this book, too.

Third, in order to create supportive contexts for children, professional development should include hands-on skill-building using these strategies and be provided to all members of the school community, including administrators, educators, mental health providers, parents, and specialists.

Fourth, these strategies must be utilized directly in classrooms with the goal of improving academic success.

Fifth, the strategies in this book should also be utilized during art, music, physical education, and other activities. Nonacademic activities often serve as bridge that can help students move from an area where they feel confident into an area, such as academics, that may be more challenging.

Finally, the strategies in this book should serve as a jumping off point for reviewing schoolwide policies. A school communicates its trauma sensitivity through policies and protocols such as those around discipline, confidentiality, communicating with families of traumatized students, the filing of abuse and neglect reports, and protection of its students.

If we are to meet state and national educational standards, we must address the role that trauma might be playing in the difficulties many students are having with learning, relationships, and behavior at school. Susan Craig's work provides important strategies to address a key element of school reform, one that is needed to ensure the success of all children.

Susan F. Cole, M.Ed., J.D.
Director
Trauma and Learning Policy Initiative
Massachusetts Advocates for Children and Harvard Law School

REFERENCES

Cole, S.F., O'Brien, J.G., Gadd, M.G., Ristuccia, J., Wallace, D.L., & Gregory, M. (2005). *Helping traumatized children learn: Supportive school environments for children traumatized by family violence.* Boston: Massachusetts Advocates for Children.

Craig, S.E. (1992). The educational needs of children living with violence. *Phi Delta Kappan, 74*(1), 67–71.

Felitti, V.J., Anda, R.F., Nordenberg, D., Williamson, D.F., Spitz, A.M., Edwards, V., et al. (1998). Relationship of childhood abuse and household dysfunction to many of the leading causes of death in adults: The adverse childhood experiences study. *American Journal of Preventative Medicine, 14*, 245–258.

Herman, J. (1992). *Trauma and recovery.* New York: Basic Books.

Massachusetts Advocates for Children. (2008). *Helping traumatized children learn: Volume II.* Manuscript in preparation.

Preface

In the late 1970s, I was a newly appointed reading specialist when I first noticed the pattern: young, aggressive children who for no apparent reason were not learning how to read. Their socioeconomic level was similar to that of other children, and they did not meet the criteria for learning disability or mental retardation. But they were not learning, and I wanted to know why. I noted that many of these children had trouble getting along with teachers and other children. Their problems did not end with academics; they crossed all school environments.

About the same time, I began a doctoral program at the University of New Hampshire, working with faculty affiliated with the Family Research Lab. I researched the effects of exposure to family violence on children's cognitive development and learning. The findings highlighted a relationship between exposure to family violence and deficits in children's language development, memory, attention, and locus of control.

Because I was working in a public school throughout the time I was conducting this research, I immediately started thinking about whether exposure to violence played a role in the problems of the children I was seeing. I started listening more closely to their stories and the stories of their parents. Experiences that are now described as family violence were not uncommon.

In 1992 I published a theoretical paper describing the possible effects of family violence on children's learning. I suggested ways that teachers could address this issue using methods developed in response to the needs of other at-risk populations. The paper resonated with educators trying to teach children whose life histories included exposure to violence. I began working with administrators, teachers, teaching assistants, and school-based mental health workers to increase their awareness of the problem of family violence and its possible consequences for children.

Subsequent magnetic resonance imaging (MRI) research that maps the effects of stress and violence on children's neural development provides empirical evidence to support my initial theories. Family violence is now discussed more openly and clinically within the educational arena, as its differential effects on children continue to be explored.

Reaching and Teaching Children Who Hurt: Strategies for Your Classroom makes no claim to resolve the diagnostic complexities of childhood trauma. Rather, it provides teachers with an overview of the broad range of developmental issues associated with exposure to family violence, and it offers ideas about how to engage and instruct children in a trauma-sensitive manner.

My hope is that this book will become a useful resource for teachers. They are the professionals who have always been on the front line in dealing with the effects of trauma on children, and they continue to have the greatest opportunity to help children overcome adversity in a life-affirming and resilient manner.

Acknowledgments

Just as children dealing with the traumatizing effects of family violence require the support of others, so to do those writing about their problems and concerns. I am grateful for the interest and concern of my family and dear friends who encouraged me to pursue my efforts to establish a relationship between children's traumatizing experiences and their inability to do well in school. Throughout the many years that it took to conceptualize and develop this manuscript, they listened patiently as I described new research that helped make the connection between trauma, neurodevelopment, and children's learning. They forgave missed telephone calls and frequent absences when research or on-site observations and program development required hours of study or time away from home. When progress was slow, they were quick to offer encouragement and refused to let me give up.

In addition to family and friends, professional colleagues were a great source of support. I am particularly thankful to the many administrators, teachers, teaching assistants, and school mental health professionals with whom I have worked and from whom I have learned. Their compassion and creativity are a source of inspiration to me as we struggle together to find better ways of caring for children and helping them succeed.

Special thanks to Rebecca Lazo of Paul H. Brookes Publishing Co. for recognizing the need for this book, as well as those who helped me develop, organize, and edit this manuscript. These individuals include Margaret Evans and Linda Desmarais for their research assistance, Kevin Craig and Marcia Chappell for reading and editing each chapter, and Ann G. Haggart, whose support, as well as her painstaking attention to detail, contributed greatly to the quality and readability of the manuscript.

1

Family Violence

A Problem of Epidemic Proportions

Exposure to violence is so prevalent in children's lives that it is a public health epidemic (Osofsky & Osofsky, 1999). Each year an alarming number of children are either witnesses to, or victims of, family violence—enduring experiences so horrifying that their lives are changed forever (Groves, 2002). This chapter highlights the needs of children dealing with the traumatizing consequences of family violence. It introduces topics that are addressed in greater detail throughout the text: the effects of trauma on children's development and the role teachers and schools can play in helping children overcome this adversity in their lives.

Daeshawn was in foster care the year I had him in my fifth-grade class. He was new to our school. It was his third placement that year. His foster placement kept changing, and every time he moved he switched schools. He acted like he didn't expect to stay long. He avoided the other children and was pretty wary of me as well.

The school psychologist told me to give Daeshawn a lot of space. She said that he had been removed from his home after a neighbor reported seeing his mother beat him with a belt in the doorway of their apartment. He and his sister were removed from her custody and separated from one another. He blamed himself for the breakup of his family and worried constantly about his mother's and sister's safety.

PREVALENCE OF THE PROBLEM

What You Know	You know that some children are victims of child abuse or other forms of family violence.
What's New	It is more likely than not that there are children in your classroom trying to manage the traumatizing consequences of family violence.

Family violence is by far the most prevalent and devastating source of childhood trauma, affecting many more children than other sources such as accidents, disasters, and medical conditions. The National Child Traumatic Stress Network (NCTSN, 2003) reported that one out of every two children seen by NCTSN mental health workers suffers from trauma caused by psychological maltreatment, traumatic loss, dependence on an impaired caregiver, or domestic violence. One in three suffers from trauma caused by sexual maltreatment and neglect (Spinazzola, Blaustein, & van der Kolk, 2005). The 1998 Adverse Childhood Experiences study further underscores the severity of the problem. Using retrospective interviews of 17,000 members of a well-known health maintenance organization (HMO), the study found that 44% of respondents reported histories of child abuse, and another 12.5% cited incidents of violence against their mothers (Felitti et al., 1998).

Estimates vary as to the exact number of children worldwide who are exposed to family violence, but the consensus is that this is a widespread problem (United Nations Children's Fund & The Bodyshop International, 2006). In the United States, child welfare agencies receive more than 3 million annual allegations of childhood abuse and neglect and collect sufficient evidence to substantiate more than 1 million of them (Teicher, Anderson, Polcari, Anderson, & Navalta, 2002).

Although these numbers are shocking, they do not tell the whole story. Teachers and others who work with children know that many children exposed to family violence are never brought to the attention of child welfare agencies. The fact is that each year hundreds of thousands of children in the United States are maltreated or victimized in their families in some manner (Perry, 2006). These children come to school unhappy and out of control. Their behavior interferes with their relationships and limits their ability to learn, whereas their stories threaten to change forever the comforting belief that age insulates children from the effects of violence.

The prevalence of family violence and its traumatizing consequences for children means that schools can no longer consider it a rare occurrence with minimal impact on children's behavior and academic success (Dyregrov, 2004; Horsman, 2000; Levine & Kline, 2007). The widespread nature of the problem demands that the needs of traumatized children be considered an integral part of all instructional planning. Schools can no longer limit interventions to individual children with known trauma histories but must create instructional frameworks that integrate a trauma-sensitive approach into all aspects of the school day.

THE TRAUMATIZING EFFECTS OF VIOLENCE ON CHILDREN'S DEVELOPMENT

What You Know	You know that children's relationships and family environment influence development.
What's New	Family violence has traumatizing effects that limit children's ability to acquire the competencies required for school success.

Until recently little was known about the effects of violence and stress on children's development. Although some authors argued that the use of corporal punishment or physical force against children is linked to various problems in development (Cohen & Brook, 1995; Sears, Maccoby, & Lewin, 1957; Straus, 2006; Straus & Stewart, 1999), it was not until the 1990s that the traumatic consequences of family violence were clearly identified (Herman, 1992; Perry & Pollard, 1998; van der Kolk & MacFarlane, 1996). It is now known that early exposure to violence, or chronic stress, alters the structure and chemistry of children's brains in predictable ways (Jensen, 1998b; Perry & Pollard, 1998; Schore, 1994; Teicher et al., 2002). Attachment relationships marred by violence and abuse threaten children's safety and destroy their sense of trust and well-being. Violence denies children the mediating presence of a caring adult who interprets their experiences for them and helps them acquire strategies for anticipating and responding to everyday problems. As a result, these children often fail to acquire the self-regulatory behaviors and social competencies necessary for academic success (Cole, O'Brien, Gadd, Ristuccia, Wallace, & Gregory, 2005). They come into school unfocused, frightened, and out of control.

Psychological Effects

When children suffer the traumatizing effects of family violence, they lose the protection of the adult world (Adler, 1994). Parents and other caregivers that they have relied on to love and protect them become the source of pain, danger, and shame. The result is an overwhelming sense of terror that makes it difficult for them to live up to the normal demands of childhood (California Attorney General's Office, 2002; Herman, 1992). Although children's reactions to this betrayal vary, they always include deep feelings of helplessness and isolation that, for most, are difficult to overcome. The intense fear of annihilation that accompanies the original trauma produces changes in children's stress responses and expectations of interpersonal relationships. These adaptations, although protective in origin, become dysfunctional over time (Solomon, 2003). For example, children may develop a distorted logic that seeks to explain, if not control, the reality of their lives, or they may become so preoccupied with safety and survival that they are unable to focus on classroom instruction or acquire new skills.

Children traumatized by family violence are put in the position of developing a trusting relationship with adults who threaten their physical safety and psychological integrity (Herman, 1992). Because it is an untenable situation, children go to great lengths to deny its reality. Some children construct explanations of the violence that make *themselves*, rather than caregivers, responsible. They minimize the dangerousness of their parents' actions by assuming these are "normal" reactions to their own misbehavior. This allows children to direct their attention toward controlling the parents' behavior, or correcting their own, rather than acknowledging the trauma they have experienced.

This denial causes the intense feelings associated with the trauma to "go underground" and makes it difficult for the children to process their feelings and move on. Their intense feelings remain, often intruding into their consciousness as disconnected visual images or physical sensations (Siegel, 1999). In the absence of a story to explain them, these unresolved feelings often erupt in angry and aggressive ways that cause problems with teachers and peers. Unable to integrate what has happened to them, these children remain locked in an internal, often unconscious, struggle to resolve the past, rather than attending to current and future realities.

Physiological Effects

Early exposure to violence organizes the brain in a manner that makes it hyperalert to danger (Jensen, 1998b; Kotulak, 1996; Perry & Pollard, 1998; Teicher et al., 2002). The hyperarousal that results is chronic and often unbearable. Anxiety and hypervigilance make it difficult for children to concentrate and limit their ability to regulate their behavior or control their emotions. Uncared for by others, these children live in a state of constant fear, ready to defend and protect themselves against danger that might occur at any time. Some resort to aggressive, acting-out behaviors, whereas others, overwhelmed by fear and loss, become unresponsive and disconnected from themselves and other people (Diamond & Hopson, 1998; Margolin & Gordis, 2000; Perry, 1994). Even when children find ways to justify or explain the damage that violence inflicts on the attachment relationship, they cannot reverse its physiological effects on their neural development.

Daeshawn was so nervous! He couldn't sit still for a minute, always jumping out of his seat to sharpen his pencil or get something out of his book bag. One day we had a fire drill and he nearly jumped out of his skin. I couldn't calm him down for the rest of the day. He had a hard time concentrating, especially when we were doing seat work and everything was quiet. He'd put his head down and pretend he was sleeping. He didn't like it when I asked him if he needed help. He'd act angry, but I think he was embarrassed that I was calling attention to him.

Cognitive Effects

Children traumatized by family violence often fail to develop a framework for learning that helps them organize their thoughts and plan for their future (Pynoos, Steinberg, & Goenjian, 1996). The unpredictable nature of their lives and the inconsistency of their care deprive them of the cognitive infrastructure needed to bring order and meaning. As a result, they often lack a basic, conceptual understanding of the world, making it difficult for them to benefit from academic instruction. This lack of conceptual framework explains many of their typical characteristics, such as the inability to understand rules or explain the reasons behind emotional outbursts or acting out behaviors.

CONSEQUENCES OF UNRESOLVED TRAUMA ON CHILDREN'S SELF-DEFINITION

What You Know	You know that supports exist to address the needs of children with behavior problems.
What's New	Trauma is sometimes camouflaged by other behavior problems. When children traumatized by family violence are misdiagnosed, they do not receive the interventions they need.

The silence that shrouds the secrets of family violence is reflected in society's response to its victims. Children often find themselves being inadvertently blamed for behaviors that occur as a response to horrible things that have been done to them. This is particularly true when reactions to trauma include externalizing behaviors that do not meet the standard for a mental health diagnosis. Even when the severity of their symptoms does result in a mental health diagnosis, such as attention-deficit/hyperactivity disorder, posttraumatic stress disorder, or conduct disorder, the full range of problems faced by traumatized children is not acknowledged. In fact, the consequences of these diagnoses often have powerful negative effects on traumatized children. These may include placement in a segregated educational setting (Levine & Kline, 2007), interventions that do not address the core issues driving their relentless behavior (Perry, 2006), or reinforcement of their internal states of helplessness and despair (Long, 1998).

Creating a more trauma-sensitive response to the needs of these children requires a better understanding of the reality of their lives. In order to help children overcome the effects of family violence teachers must acknowledge that such violence exists. Children need to know that teachers understand that violence sometimes happens in families and that they know how to keep children safe. Children need to know that they are not alone but are surrounded by a team of caring and competent adults who can help them overcome the barriers to learning that result from trauma.

I remember going to a workshop on child abuse and neglect. I expected it to be about the teacher's role as a mandated reporter. Instead, the presenter talked about the prevalence of child abuse and how it affects children's development. She reviewed the statistics and then looked up at the audience and said,

> *These children are in your classrooms. They come to school every day looking for someone who will acknowledge what they are going through and offer to help them out. I don't mean that they want you to violate their family's confidentiality or abandon your role as teacher to become a social worker or counselor. Children don't need that from you. But what they do need is for you to be on their side. They need you to understand that their inappropriate behavior is a cry for help, even when it seems to be a personal attack or an act of defiance. These children are fighting for their lives. They need you to know enough about trauma to accommodate to their needs and partner with them*

to acquire the self-regulatory behaviors they need to be success-
ful at school.

Her statements really got my attention. None of the other workshops I
had attended on child abuse ever talked about what teachers could do
to help the children out. Even when I had children in my classroom who
I knew were living with violence, no one ever talked to me about how
that affected their learning or how I could help them overcome those
effects. It was like none of us wanted to know.

Trauma is not an event in itself but, rather, a response to an experience that is so stressful that it overwhelms an individual's capacity to cope. When supportive adults are readily available and safety can be quickly restored, the traumatic effects of violence on children are greatly mitigated (Osofsky & Fenichel, 1994). However, when trauma is left unresolved, it forces children to carry relentless needs for survival and safety into environments where these needs are no longer developmentally appropriate. For some children these problems lead to unruly, aggressive behaviors that disrupt classroom activities and routines (Shonk & Cicchetti, 2001). For others, it leads to patterns of excessive perfectionism and overresponsibility, often accompanied by anxiety, depression, and self-destructive behaviors (Herman, 1992).

Although some traumatized children do well in school despite their stressful home environments, many do not (Craig, 1992; Groves, 2002; Osofsky & Osofsky, 1999). Traumatized children often receive lower grades and poorer scores on standardized tests and other measures of academic achievement (Cook et al., 2007). They are more frequently referred for special education services (Jonson-Reid, 2004) and may also fail to develop adequate literacy skills, as indicated by the high number of participants in adult literacy classes who report past histories of family or domestic violence (Horsman, 2000). Students who experience trauma are at increased risk for dropping out of school (Cook et al., 2007; Widom, 2000) and are more likely than peers to engage in delinquent behavior before adolescence (Petit & Brooks, 1998).

HOW SCHOOLS CAN HELP

What You Know	You know that enriching school experiences have a positive effect on at-risk children.
What's New	Once you know how violence affects children's behavior, you can work proactively to accommodate to their needs.

The social support available in schools can help children exposed to violence restore trust in themselves and others (Harvey, 1996). Schools are unique in that they can provide children with long-term support in recovering from the traumatizing effects of family violence. The length of the school day and options for summer and after-school programs give children repeated opportunities for healing within a context of caring relationships and age-appropriate activities.

Positive school experiences engender the feelings of safety and belonging that traumatized children crave. When schools anticipate the needs of these children and support their participation in classrooms with other children, they are able to avoid the stigmatizing effects of segregated placements or out-of-control behavior. Within the social context of the school, children find the courage and freedom to expand their experience and discover new interests and talents.

The predictable schedule and routine of the school day helps children acquire a conceptual understanding of the world, organize their experiences in meaningful ways, and bring order to the chaos of their daily lives (Craig, 1992). When trauma-sensitive interventions are integrated into daily activities and routines, children get the support and guidance they need throughout the day, *every* day, rather than once or twice a week in a clinical setting (Perry, 2006). This allows them the time and the practice they need to correct distorted assumptions about themselves and to establish their ability to exert some control over their lives. Opportunities for safe, predictable interactions with others help them reconnect with adults as sources of support and understanding.

I really wanted Daeshawn to be able to go to art, music, and physical education, but I was concerned that the classes would be too unstructured for him. I was afraid he might have a meltdown if he got confused by the rules or didn't understand the routine. He wouldn't mean to get in trouble, but his anxiety might get the best of him.

I talked to the school psychologist about it and she recommended trying rehearsal strategies with Daeshawn. We decided it would help Daeshawn to observe the different classes before he attended them. So the psychologist went with Daeshawn and they observed what was going on in each class. They both took notes about what they saw. Then they met to review their notes and develop a list of "required behaviors" for each class. Together, they determined which ones Daeshawn might need to practice or improve on, as well as any additional supports Daeshawn thought he'd need.

Daeshawn decided that he wanted me to check in with him before each of the "specials." If he was feeling particularly anxious or out of control he could opt to stay in the classroom. Otherwise, he didn't think he needed any additional support. That was several weeks ago, and he's doing fine. He seems to really enjoy the classes and the teachers are enjoying him. Giving him a heads up on what to expect was all he needed.

Appropriate Supports

Moderating the effects of trauma on children's development and helping them acquire social and academic competencies requires schools to establish and adhere to appropriate supports that are responsive to the physical, cognitive, and emotional aspects of trauma. These include an empathic response to children's needs, teacher–student collaboration to ensure safety and manage stress, and school policies that reflect a trauma sensitive approach.

Responding Empathically to Children's Needs

Traumatized children are vulnerable to the judgments of others. They have limited resources to cope with the trauma of family violence and cannot risk being misunderstood. In school they rely on teachers to "read" and interpret their needs for safety, support, and self-regulation (Levine & Kline, 2007). The responses teachers make to children's behavior have a powerful effect on children's ability to resolve a traumatic past. Teachers help children discover new talents or ambitions, and they support the development of affective and instrumental competencies. A teacher's support in regulating behavior and managing emotions helps children develop confidence in the ability of adults to care about them and keep them safe. When teachers interpret children's behaviors empathetically, they work to contain problematic behavior rather than further escalate it. Teachers also guide children to build on experiences of self-regulation and develop more adaptive responses to problems rather than reacting in an impulsive, thoughtless manner. This type of reparative experience with a teacher helps children reestablish their trust in people and learn to experience relationships as a source of comfort and relaxation (Garbarino, Dubrow, Kostelny, & Pardo, 1992).

One year I worked with a music teacher who really knew how to connect with children. We called him our "turnaround teacher" because of all the times he was able to motivate children and get them on the right track. He told a story about a high school student who was on the verge of dropping out. He was in trouble with everyone. Some of the teachers thought he might run away because things were pretty hard at home— no money, lots of alcohol, and who knows what else. Anyway, this teacher met him in the music room one day after school. He was fooling around with the keyboard. The teacher offered to give him lessons a few times a week. That was 2 years ago. The boy turned out to have a lot of musical talent. He stayed in school, cleaned up his act, and last week won a scholarship to the Berklee College of Music in Boston. Stories like that make you remember why you became a teacher.

Maintaining an empathic response to traumatized children requires teachers to rethink common assumptions about the motivations underlying children's behavior. Most behavior management systems are based on the assumption that children are able to adapt and tolerate frustration well enough to change their behaviors in compliance with classroom expectations (Greene & Ablon, 2006). Misbehaviors are within the child's control; they can choose how they wish to behave (Watson & Westby, 2003). This is not always the case for traumatized children. Their apparent "opposition/defiance, aggression, emotional disengagement, and avoidance of responsibility" are often produced by traumatic stress reactions over which they have little control (Henry, Sloane, & Black-Pond, 2007, p. 106). As a result, using *consequences* to achieve compliance with school or classroom rules is *seldom effective*, and may, in fact, escalate negative behaviors when children are unable to comply for reasons neither they nor their teacher understand.

Collaborative Partnerships

Responding to the needs of children traumatized by family violence requires a clear understanding of their internal states. Traumatized children are afraid. Fear drives their behavior and limits their capacity to function. Intrusive memories of traumatic events, or unbearable feelings of fear and anger, result in rapid changes in mood and activity level that are better managed through teacher–child collaboration than through more traditional, authoritarian approaches.

These partnerships start with helping the children control the symptoms of hyperarousal, the body's physiological and emotional response to danger. Teachers carefully observe of children's behavior and provide the support needed to help them remain relaxed and interested in what is going on around them. As students come to rely on teachers to help them recognize and contain overwhelming feelings, challenging behaviors are used as an opportunity to teach more adaptive responses. These nurturing experiences with a caring adult help children change their beliefs about themselves. They begin to question the internal message, "I am defective, destructive, and unlovable," that results from relational trauma. Relationships with adults are viewed as the source of comfort and support—an important step in overcoming the traumatizing legacy of family violence.

I remember that when I first started teaching it was really hard for me to understand my role in managing children's behavior. I think I had some pretty unrealistic expectations that were probably not developmentally appropriate. I was so focused on making them accountable for their behavior that I seldom tried to understand a situation from their point of view.

One day I was complaining to my principal about the disruptive behavior of one of my children. Her response was, "Children do the best they can. What can you change about your teaching practice to help this child be more successful?" At first I was kind of annoyed, but as I thought about it, I knew she was right. Children don't want to be seen as disruptive and noncompliant. If they act out, it's their way of signaling that something in the environment exceeds their capacity to cope. It's my job to figure out what that is and improve the situation by changing the environment or improving the child's skills.

Managing Stress

Helping children manage stress begins with a safe, caring classroom environment where children are accepted and respected for who they are. Developmentally appropriate activities and the mediating presence of a caring, competent adult creates a context where children learn to manage the physical symptoms of stress. Patterned, repetitive sensory input such as music, dance, deep breathing, or drumming can be integrated into classroom activities as a way of inducing relaxation and increasing children's capacity to learn (Perry, 2006).

The sense of well-being that results from improved regulation of the body's stress response gives children enough security and clarity to begin acquiring more functional ways of coping with adversity. These include strategies that increase their self-awareness and provide them with opportunities for choice making and self-reflection throughout the day. Coupled with opportunities for physical movement and emotional support, these strategies help children contain the fear associated with childhood trauma and use their energy in more enjoyable and productive ways.

School Policies

When schools take a systemic approach to meeting the needs of children traumatized by family violence, they proactively plan for possible problems. School administrators may find it necessary to modify some policies to reflect a better understanding of the prevalence of childhood trauma and its potential impact on children's learning and behavior. In particular, policies pertaining to safety planning, discipline, and community collaboration may need to be scrutinized and changed.

Safety Planning

Acknowledging the reality of family violence and its traumatizing effect on children is inseparable from instituting policies that ensure the safety of staff and of families affected by violence. These policies include ascertaining which families have court orders preventing contact or the exchange information and having protocols in place to keep children's personal information out of the hands of perpetrators. Staff should know that they are prohibited from disclosing information about children to parents against whom restraining orders or other domestic court orders have been issued. They should understand district policies about transferring records and removing identifying contact information from documents before releasing these documents to a noncustodial parent.

Discipline

Children traumatized by family violence often have little experience with rules or expectations of behavior that are intended to protect them and ensure their well-being. These children are easily frightened and may interpret any attempt to control their behavior as a threat to their safety. They respond best to codes of conduct or expectations of behavior that are developed cooperatively and reviewed on a regular basis to assess their effectiveness in maintaining a safe, cooperative learning environment.

Discipline policies need to acknowledge the kinds of problem behaviors children may exhibit, and supports should be put in place to limit their occurrence. Positive relationships with teachers and school administrators should be used as a context in which to address the behaviors of individual children through positive behavior support (PBS) and individualized behavior intervention plans (Cole et al., 2005). The discipline code of the school must be understood as a contract between adults and children to maintain a safe, violence-free environment where children get what they need to learn and be successful.

Community Collaboration

Helping children cope with trauma requires a network of support services used to address concerns that cannot be addressed during the school day: community mental health programs, after-school child care programs, and social service agencies that are available to families in emergencies. Schools should have protocols in place for creating good working relationships with community resources, such as appointing a staff member as a liaison to community organizations and involving school personnel in wraparound services for children.

CONCLUSION

Extensive work remains to be done in understanding and facilitating the educational achievement of children exposed to violence. Ultimately, the best solution for the educational difficulties of traumatized children is the elimination of family violence. Until then, recognition of the problems faced by these children and the role that schools can play to promote academic and social competence will help reduce a host of harmful consequences.

2

Exposure to Violence Changes How Children Learn

Children exposed to violence approach learning differently than their peers. Exposure to violence distorts children's perceptions of themselves and others. These distortions, coupled with poor impulse control, interfere with effective problem solving. This chapter describes how schools can accommodate these cognitive characteristics by using academic instruction to build resilience and hope in traumatized children.

Mark's father is in jail for assault, and Mark's mother seems very overwhelmed. She's always losing her job or getting sick. Trouble just seems to follow that family. And it shows in Mark. He is one of the saddest children I've met. He is always telling me that nothing ever goes right for him. If he makes a mistake or I have to correct something in his work, he just gives up! He crosses his arms in front of him and looks down. He's his own worst critic. I wish there were some way I could help Mark lighten up a little.

Mark behaves a lot like children with attention-deficit/hyperactivity disorder. He is impulsive and has a hard time getting things done. The slightest change in the schedule really gets him upset. He has trouble attending to what is going on in the classroom, often spacing out and losing track of what he's supposed to be doing. Mark's also pretty defensive with the other children. It's like he has this chip on his shoulder. He can't let go of anything he sees as unfair. He persists on going over the same slight or insult again and again.

IMPACT ON CHILDREN'S FEELINGS AND PERCEPTIONS

What You Know	You know that children's early experiences shape how they think about themselves and others.
What's New	Exposure to violence distorts children's perceptions of themselves and others in ways that interfere with the development of higher order thinking and perspective taking.

Exposure to violence affects how children feel about learning, how they think, and how they behave. Patterns of learned helplessness and lack of control make it difficult for them to participate in classroom activities. Their focus on safety and survival limits the ability to concentrate and to acquire higher order thinking skills. They are subject to hyperarousal and persistent states of fear and anxiety, which put self-reflection and critical thinking outside their reach.

Mark has to know everything that is going on in the classroom. If we have a visitor, he wants to know why the person is there. If a child is absent, he wants to know when that student is coming back. He's always watching me, trying to gauge my mood or anticipate my response to him. I remind him that he's safe, but he can't let down his guard. It's like he's waiting for things to fall apart.

Higher Order Thinking

Learning involves thinking as well as processing information. Early experiences shape children's assumptions about how the world works. Repeated experiences of safety, belonging, and respect result in positive assumptions about the world, whereas experiences of neglect, rejection, and disrespect lead to more negative outcomes. By the time children reach school age they have developed a characteristic way of thinking about themselves and what goes on around them. This "explanatory narrative" shapes how children explain what happens to them. It places them within their own life story, defining who they are and what they are capable of. The explanatory narrative determines how children direct and sustain their attention, how they define and resolve the problems they encounter, and how they monitor and change their behavior to achieve goals (Cozolino, 2006). It defines children's understanding of their relationship to others and how their behavior affects others reactions to them.

Children exposed to violence, particularly within the context of parental abuse, often distort the reality of their situation in ways that make learning difficult. As noted in Chapter 1, some children explain the parent's wrongdoing as a justifiable reaction to their own "badness" (Siegel, 2007; van der Kolk, 2001). The underlying distortion is that the child, not the parent, is responsible for the abuse. Some children resort to patterns of behavior that reinforce the notion of their intrinsic badness by creating problems in both school and community. Others try to correct their badness by adopting rigid patterns of perfectionist behavior. They attempt to do whatever is required of them as perfectly as possible (Herman, 1992). In both cases, the explanatory narrative developed by these children is riddled with pessimism, frustration, and lack of control. Life happens to them rather than being shaped by them. They react rather than respond. They often lack a clear understanding of cause and effect, which limits their ability to think proactively. Focused on controlling the behavior of others, they are unable to fully develop the self-awareness required for perspective taking and problem solving.

Perspective Taking

Children exposed to violence often carry cognitive distortions, developed as a defense against abusive parenting, into relationships with peers and adults. They constantly adjust their perceptions to match past experiences. They often interpret innocuous stimuli as threatening and see anger in faces that are neutral, sad, or ambiguous (Pollack, Klorman, Thatcher, & Cicchetti, 2001; Pollack & Tolley-Schell, 2003). Limited self-awareness coupled with few opportunities to explore their thoughts and perceptions with caring adults makes understanding another person's point of view difficult. As a result, these children have trouble with social activities, such as cooperative play and social conversation. They also have trouble making inferences to explain or predict other people's behavior.

The school psychologist and I are trying to help Mark get better at seeing situations from other people's point of view. Not being able to put himself into somebody else's shoes really limits his ability to play games or get along with the other children. It also affects how well he can predict what a character in a story is going to do. So we've been playing this game with Mark and the other children: We have the students work in teams of two to describe a situation—first from one child's point of view, then from the other's point of view. We also have them describe things from the perspective of "now versus then" and "here versus there." I think it's really helping all of the children become a little bit more flexible and better able to see someone else's point of view.

What You Can Do

- Play the "perspective taking game." After reading a section of a story or watching part of a video that focuses on the main character, stop and ask the children what they think one of the minor characters is thinking or feeling based on what you've read or seen. Continue the story to find out whose idea is closest to the truth for the character (Seligman, Reivich, Joycox, & Gillham, 1995).

- If you are having a conflict with a child, switch roles for a minute so that each person can understand why the other is acting that way (Seligman et al., 1995).

- Design lessons using the Role, Audience, Form, Topic (RAFT) strategy. In discussing a topic, assign children different roles, ask them to address different audiences, and discuss the story from these varying perspectives (Rutherford, 2002).

- When reading a story, encourage children to listen for a character's point of view. Ask them how their point of view is the same as or different from that of the character.
- Have children stand in different parts of the room and draw or describe what they see from that perspective. Help them notice the different ways of perceiving the same situation.

What Do You Think?

Mr. Drury works in an elementary school located in the same community as the state prison. Several of the children in his first-grade classroom have parents who are incarcerated. He is particularly concerned about one girl, Jessica, who works really hard but can never seem to take pleasure in her accomplishments. The children tease her about being too perfect and never making any mistakes. Mr. Drury wants to help Jessica lighten up a little and relax but isn't sure about what to do. What would you tell him?

a   Congratulate Jessica on her ability to stay focused on schoolwork, despite what is going on at home. Let her help you correct papers and do other "teacher tasks" to help her feel accepted and cared for.

b   Tell Jessica to ignore the children who are making fun of her. Let them know that you wish more of them would apply themselves the way she does.

c   Involve Jessica in cooperative games and group projects where she can learn how to relax and play with other children.

The correct answer is (c). Jessica needs help learning that other people can be sources of support and understanding. In turn, she needs a teacher who will create opportunities for her to get to know the other children and learn how to interact with them. Mr. Drury is correct in recognizing Jessica's need to relax. Her perfectionist behavior is indicative of the stress she is feeling. Mr. Drury needs to be careful not to reinforce her already high expectations of herself by allowing her to assume a parental-type role (a) or by inadvertently holding her up as an example to other children (b).

IMPACT ON CHILDREN'S EXPERIENCES WITH SUCCESS

What You Know	You know that children who are depressed or pessimistic about their ability to succeed sometimes lack the motivation and persistence they need to master academic tasks.
What's New	Frequent experiences of feeling out of control make children who have been exposed to violence pessimistic about their ability to succeed or improve their situation in any way.

Having been so unsuccessful in controlling events in the past, children with histories of violence and relational trauma are pessimistic about the future. Because they have grown up with parents whose unrealistic expectations and explosive behavior makes failing dangerous, these children fear being in situations where they do not know what to do (Morrow, 1987). Fear of being seen as incapable makes it difficult for them to ask for help or to seek reassurance from teachers. Some withdraw, whereas others develop patterns of noncompliance or not completing work as "face-saving" techniques to hide their vulnerability. Although these behaviors are painful in themselves, the children believe that it is safer to engage in them than to experience failure in front of teachers and peers.

Most children expect teachers and other adults to help them out when they are struggling to learn something new. They ask questions and watch as you form a letter of the alphabet or download a picture for the cover of their book report. They seek you out when someone has hurt their feelings, or when they need reassurance. But not Mark. He never asks for help. Even when you offer, he'll refuse to let you show him how something works or where to go to get the information he needs. It's like he thinks he needs to know everything. Asking for help would be like exposing a weakness he's not willing to admit to.

What You Can Do

- Make sure that classroom expectations are developmentally appropriate. When children are given meaningful tasks that they are capable of doing, they often feel more in control of themselves.
- Teach children how to think out loud about the resources that they can use to solve a problem or reach a goal. Display a running list of available resources on wall space or a bulletin board. For example, who are the people who can help them solve a school-based problem such as getting playground equipment or changing the cafeteria menu? Where could children get ideas about how other people solved a similar problem? What could they read to get new ideas?
- Have a buddy system in your classroom that allows children to rely on one another to get the help they need and feel successful. Pair children up by complementary strengths to complete assignments.
- Model asking for help. Talk about how different people at the school were able to help you do things that you needed to get accomplished. For example, the school secretary mailed some letters for you, and the custodian helped you get your car started. Help children see that it is all right to ask for and receive help and support from other people.

IMPACT ON CONCEPT DEVELOPMENT

What You Know	You know that children need to have an understanding of basic concepts to understand and apply what they learn in school.
What's New	Children living with family violence are often deprived of the experiences they need to acquire basic concepts such as cause and effect and sequencing.

Most children learn about cause and effect by actively exploring the world around them. They quickly learn that they can make things happen, and this understanding gives them the foundation for developing a sense of competence and responsibility. They become the locus of control in their own lives—responsible, at least in part, for both their successes and their failures.

I want Mark to feel like he has more control over what happens to him, that what he does makes a difference. He never seems to see the relationship between what he does and how things turn out. If things are going well and he's having a good day, he says he's just lucky. If things go wrong or he gets in trouble for something he's done, he blames someone else or says it's not fair. How can he ever take pride in himself if he can't see the effect of his actions?

Children living with violence often have histories of physical restriction and unrealistic parental expectations that inhibit their exploration of the world and their emergent sense of competence. Experience has taught them that violence erupts unpredictably, with no consistent, comprehensible cause. Particularly in an abusive situation, when a parent might respond to the same neutral act sometimes with rancor and sometimes with praise, children do not learn how to anticipate events or predict outcomes based on past experiences. This distorts the perception of their potential to make things happen or affect what goes on around them. As a result they often fail to develop a clear understanding of cause-and-effect relationships (Craig, 1992; Perry, 2002). This inability to make causal connections carries over into children's academic life; they struggle to negotiate tasks that rely on hypothesis testing and have difficulty learning from their mistakes. Experiencing life as out of their control, they often lack the motivation to persist at academic tasks. It is difficult for them to learn how to set goals or delay gratification. Many are unable to benefit from behavior management techniques that assume an understanding of cause and effect.

Token economies and other types of behavior modification really don't work very well with children exposed to violence. They just don't get the connection between what they are doing and your response. That was so clear to me the other day when the principal stopped in my classroom.

She walked around the room, talking quietly to individual children, telling them they were doing a good job. As she was leaving, she spoke to the whole class, telling them she was so proud of how they were working that she was going to send down some special stickers. Mark looked up at me and said, "Boy, she must be in a really good mood today, if she's giving us stickers. She never does that when she's in a bad mood or mad." I thought to myself, "There's the distortion. What happens to you isn't the result of what you are doing, like working hard. It's all about what mood the adult is in."

What You Can Do

- Provide children with "if . . . then" scripts that encourage them to anticipate possible outcomes of a behavior they are exhibiting: "If I study hard, then I'll pass my test" or "If I exercise every day, then I'll grow strong."
- Encourage children to set a social and/or academic goal each day. These can be written on special goal sheets that children keep on their desks. For example, one child may have the goal "Keep my hands to myself." Another might be working on the goal "Remember to check for spelling errors in written work." Check in with children several times daily to see how they are doing. If they are struggling, talk about the kinds of supports you or a classmate can provide. Have some way of marking or acknowledging when the goal is met.
- Prior to reading a story aloud, ask the children to make predictions about what will happen in the text. As you read through the story, use sticky notes to mark the sentences that substantiate or negate the hypothesis. Chart the results for the class to see.
- Encourage children to evaluate the choices they make in relation to the desired outcome. This might be accomplished through a teacher–student discussion— for example, "You thought you could get your science project done if you worked with Jorge. How did it go? Did you meet your goal, or do you wish you'd made a different choice?"
- Offer children opportunities to choose from among a variety of strategies to complete an assignment by asking, for example, "Do you want to use a graphic organizer or an outline to organize your paragraph?" (Doll, Sands, Wehmeyer, & Palmer, 1996).

What Do You Think?

Mr. Chris works in a rural school. He knows that many of his students have histories of family violence. He wants to make a difference but struggles with what to do. What would you tell him?

a   Exposure to violence can affect children's behavior in ways that are best dealt with by school psychologists. There is not much you can do in the classroom. Get as many of these students into counseling as possible.

b   Children exposed to violence need to feel safe. Stick to skill and drill instruction that does not threaten them. Otherwise they might feel incompetent and lose control.

c   Children exposed to violence need repeated opportunities to discover cause-and-effect relationships. Design instruction that teaches students to generate and test hypotheses in a supportive, caring environment.

The correct answer is (c). Exposure to violence interferes with children's understanding of cause and effect. Limited opportunities for higher order thinking (b) do not give these children the opportunity to develop a conceptual understanding of the world. Although some children benefit from counseling (a), traumatized children have cognitive issues that need to be addressed within a classroom setting. They need access to quality curriculum and instruction.

Sequencing

The ability to learn things sequentially allows children to complete tasks in an efficient, logical manner and to bring linear order to otherwise chaotic daily experiences. The ability to retain information in a linear sequence of past, present, and future enables them to use previously learned information to set goals, plan for future events, or predict future outcomes.

Prior to the development of semantic language, children encode information episodically—that is, as a collection of random events rather than a coherent narrative (Cole et al., 2005). Access to familiar, reliable caregivers encourages language development within the context of consistent, predictable routines. Children then develop the capacity to remember things sequentially. They encode new information within the context of prior experience.

Children exposed to violence or other types of relational trauma are often deprived of the types of caregiving experiences that nourish the development of sequential memory. They may be raised in households in which rules and routines are subject to the whim of a parent. Experiences of powerlessness and learned helplessness disrupt these children's ability to plan, anticipate, and hope (Lubit, Rovine, Defrancisci, & Eth, 2003). Living within family systems focused on the "now," with little emphasis on past or future, children find classroom environments that rely on sequential ordering difficult. They have difficulty organizing and processing the content of academic instruction for later retrieval and application.

Mark seems frozen in "now." He doesn't seem to recognize patterns of experiences. It's as though he's learning everything for the first time, even when we are following a routine or practicing a skill that we have been working on for months. It's like he can't link new information to existing categories or prior knowledge. It must be so frustrating for him. As his teacher, it is for me, too.

The school psychologist and speech-language pathologist are giving me strategies to help Mark understand the steps in everyday routines. They made task cards for Mark, one for each classroom activity. Each card has a picture of one step, and the cards are in the order that the steps should be completed. For instance, there's one card for getting his paper out, then one card for reading the directions, and so on. As Mark finishes a step, he's supposed to cross it out and move on to the next one. The cards are laminated and Mark uses a water soluble marker to make the checks; it takes no time to clean them so that they are ready the next time he needs to use them. So far, this approach seems to be working. He's handing work in on time and doesn't seem so frustrated.

What You Can Do

- Provide explicit instruction on a step-by-step approach to critical thinking.
- Teach children how to use self-talk to strengthen the sequential process of critical thinking.
- Give children numerous opportunities to practice sequencing events. Use time-lines, before and after pictures, and "that was then, this is now" writing exercises to order things sequentially.
- Provide opportunities for children to practice changing the sequence of everyday activities and then discuss what the experience was like. Examples include eating dessert before lunch, putting on socks over shoes, and so forth.
- Have children reverse the order of events in familiar stories.

What Do You Think?

Ms. Furlong teaches third grade in an inner-city neighborhood. Many of her students have trouble remembering to think before they act. She's tried verbal reminders, but they don't seem to work. What would you suggest?

a   Teach the children to use a cognitive strategy to create a delay between an event and their reaction to it. Agree on a word that everyone in the class will use to remember to stop and think. Post the word throughout the room and refer to it often.

b   Let the students know the consequences of their impulsive behavior. Take points off their grades or time off recess to reinforce the fact that you do not tolerate impulsive, thoughtless behaviors.

c   These students may have attention-deficit/hyperactivity disorder. Talk to the school nurse about getting the parents in touch with their physician to request an evaluation and possible medication.

The correct answer is (a). Children who exhibit impulsive behaviors need help in learning to use language to delay action so they can think about what they want to do. Teaching them how to accomplish this and offering them many opportunities to practice with you and their peers helps children develop their ability to act rather than react. Threats of consequences (b) may make it even harder for students to think clearly. Although it is true that some children do benefit from a medical diagnosis and medication (c), this approach should always be administered in concert with an educational program that helps the students become more self reflective and aware.

IMPACT ON PROBLEM-SOLVING ABILITIES

What You Know	You know that problem solving is a complex process involving judgment, decision making, and logical thought processes.
What's New	Children traumatized by family violence often react to problems rather than solving them in a thoughtful, reflective manner.

Problem solving is a quagmire for children exposed to violence. Past experiences with inconsistent caregivers and unpredictable routines impair their ability to order things sequentially or to use sequential steps to resolve a dispute. They often have little opportunity to play or to participate in other role-taking activities that are essential to developing the ability to appreciate another's point of view (van der Kolk, 2005). They find it difficult to shift their attention or hold more than one perspective on a problem. Their reasoning is inflexible, making it difficult for them to compromise or negotiate. In addition, these children seldom see themselves as capable of mobilizing resources to address the problems they encounter. Low tolerance for frustration, coupled with repeated experiences of having no control over what happens in their lives, causes them to judge things as being too hard to try or to give up at the first sign of difficulty. Giving children opportunities to see the same situation from multiple perspectives helps them learn perspective taking. Learning to recognize and appreciate "shades of gray" increases their tolerance of ambiguity.

I've finally found a strategy to help Mark get better at problem solving. I call it the "3-Ds." It involves using the same vocabulary to talk about all different sorts of problems—whether we are dealing with science or math or something that happened on the playground. First, we DEFINE what the problem is. We put it in words, sometimes writing on a big sheet of paper so we can refer back to it when the conversation gets off track. Then we DECIDE what we want to happen. This involves estimating what the possible outcomes could be. It's a great opportunity to teach children how to make predictions based on past experiences. Next, we DETERMINE what resources we need. Can we solve the problem on our own, or do we need to call in other resources? How much time do we need? What strategies will we use? Finally, we SOLVE the problem, using the strategies we have agreed on. It's a system that works because it teaches children that problems are really anything they have to make a decision about. Working together to address each step helps them learn how to think and monitor their progress toward a solution. Sometimes we have to switch strategies or go back and define the problem differently than we did in the beginning.

What You Can Do

- Have children develop work plans for projects. Work with them to develop a description of what the final product will be, including a rubric that contains its essential elements. A rubric should be developed prior to doing the project so that the child can use it as a guide (Levine, 2002b).
- When reading stories to children, stop at certain points and ask the children to predict endings. Record the predictions; when you've finished reading, compare the predictions with what actually happened.
- Use brainstorming to help children list various options for solving a problem. Record each option. Encourage children to select their preferred option. When the problem is solved, discuss the pros and cons of each selected option.
- Have children write multiple endings for stories that they are composing. Have classmates select the one they judge as most congruent with the story line.
- Wrap up each day with a class meeting in which children review the "news of the day." Have them list things that happened to them throughout the day and how they will use these experiences to solve problems or anticipate events in the future.
- Encourage children to evaluate their own performance by correcting their own papers through the use of a rubric or checklist. Encourage them to

identify any patterns of error. Plan time to work with individual children to correct these.

What Do You Think?

Mr. Foley knows that many of the children in his classroom have trouble finishing work. If the answers are not immediately apparent to these children, they give up. He wants to teach them how to improve but isn't sure how to get past their lack of persistence. What would you tell Mr. Foley?

a   The students probably just need motivation. Set up a reward system in the classroom by which children can earn points for every paper they complete. Let them use the points to earn free time or little prizes such as stickers or new pencils.

b   Use play activities like games and puzzles to help children understand the process of problem solving without worrying about academic consequences.

c   Children need to understand the consequences of their behaviors. They need to know that if they do not complete their work, their grades will suffer. Offer to hold a "catch up clinic" a few times a week during recess. If children do not take advantage of this extra help, take points off their grades.

The correct answer is (b). Many children who have trouble completing work do not have a systematic way to approach problems. They may have difficulty deciding the order in which to complete the required steps, or they may not know how to identify what the problem requires them to solve. Interpreting children's behavior as a lack of motivation (a) or offering them extra time to catch up (c) does not give them the skills they may be missing. Games and puzzles require a systematic approach. Talking about problem-solving strategies and applying them in play situations help children develop the ability to "think outside the box" and generate a variety of solutions to the same problem.

IMPACT ON ATTENTION

What You Know	You know that children's ability to attend to instruction is a strong predictor of success in school.
What's New	Exposure to violence changes children's stress response in ways that make it difficult to attend to classroom instruction.

Paying attention is essential to both learning and behavior. Attending is a complex process that allows children to learn by recognizing and responding to what is important in their environment. It includes the skills of encoding new information and reflecting on one's internal state. When children can attend to how they are thinking or feeling, they can change their explanatory narrative in response to changes in their experiences or perspective.

Mark seems to be most alive when he's living on the edge. He is always in crisis about something: he lost his milk money, he forgot his homework, he missed the bus. Part of this is because he doesn't always think about what he is doing. But it is also because he only pays attention when his emotions run high. Otherwise he barely notices what is going on. It is as if all the things he's been through reset his attention threshold. When everyday events don't match the intensity of his early experiences, important information can go unnoticed.

Attention is selective by nature, focusing first on survival and safety needs. When these most basic needs are met, our attention is directed toward making sense of the continuous stream of information that flows into consciousness. By paying attention, thoughts and experiences are organized and interpreted in meaningful ways.

The ability to regulate attention is critical to successful participation in classroom activities and routines. Teachers expect children as young as age 5 to respond to visual or verbal cues alerting them to what is important in the classroom. They are expected to direct their attention to the selected task and to sustain their attention until the task is completed.

Exposure to violence changes the structure and chemistry of children's brains in ways that make attending to classroom instruction difficult: The brain reacts to violence by developing neural pathways that are overresponsive to environmental stressors and perceptions of danger (Banks, 2001; Kotulak, 1996; Stein & Kendall, 2004). When children are beset by persistent, unbearable memories of traumatic events, both their concentration and their motivation to learn new things are impaired. Past experiences with unpredictable or dangerous adults interfere with children's ability to direct and sustain attention to critical elements of classroom instruction.

Perceptions of Danger

Hypervigilance to danger is a hallmark characteristic of children exposed to violence. Although useful in alerting children to possible threats, it interferes with the development of attending behaviors associated with school success. A near constant state of hyperarousal makes it difficult to take in new information or focus on what is being taught in the classroom (Perry, 2002; Streek-Fischer & van der Kolk, 2000). Attention downshifts to what is necessary for survival, thereby inhibiting normal curiosity and exploratory play (Hart, 1998).

Frequent downshifting of neural processes to a survival mode is one of the most significant impacts of violence on learning. The body's emotional system is designed to direct the brain to pay attention to a perceived threat before upshifting to reflective activities or higher order thinking (Niehoff, 1999). In typical development, this biological response to danger allows an individual to narrow attention to survival needs. Yet children exposed to violence often downshift in response to *neutral* stimuli (Levine & Kline, 2007). In doing so, they are physically unable to activate higher order thinking and problem solving (Sylwester, 1995)—as though all of their energy is put into ensuring their physical safety and survival even when their environments are safe. This seriously compromises the ability to attend to academic instruction, acquire new information, engage in new ideas, or expand their understanding of the world.

Intrusive Memories

Memories of traumatic events can intrude into children's consciousness, wiping out their ability to attend to less emotionally gripping activities. This results in "counterfactual thinking," the tendency to keep revisiting painful experiences with an eye toward generating alternative scenarios (Schacter, 2001, p. 165). Traumatized children are obsessed with the traumatic event and how things could have happened differently if, for example, they had only known their parents would wake up angry, if only they had known there would be a shooting at the corner store, and so forth. Beset with negative thoughts, these children acquire a ruminating explanatory style, which then traps them in patterns of self-destructive behavior that make learning all but impossible. Their mood and attention remain focused on the negative aspects of past experience, thereby limiting their motivation to explore new ideas or patterns of behavior.

Directing and Sustaining Attention

Paying attention always involves selecting from a variety of competing options. Children attend to what they have been *taught* to see. Their brains' neural networks look for patterns established by past experience. Children who have learned to look to adults as sources of information and support are therefore primed to direct their attention to what teachers *say*. They are prepared to attend to the content of instruction.

Past experiences with unpredictable, capricious adults, however, teach children to be on the lookout for hints of displeasure or emotional volatility in adults. Attention is directed toward the facial expressions and gestures that may signal danger. These children are primed to direct their attention toward what teachers *do*. They often miss the content of what is being said to them because their attention is focused on assessing the potential danger of the interaction. This seriously limits children's ability to benefit from classroom instruction. Concerns with the relational aspects of the interaction distract from the task at hand: acquiring new skills and information. The situation is often further complicated by the fact that because these children have missed the content of what is being said, they are often accused of not paying attention. This invalidates their experience, again leaving them frustrated and feeling powerless. They *were* paying attention—just to the wrong things.

Before school started this year I went to a workshop on the effects of violence on learning. The presenter talked a lot about the amygdala, this tiny little almond shaped structure in the brain that controls our reactions to stress. He said that exposure to violence "hard wires" the amygdala, causing it to be habitually on the lookout for danger. As a result, children who have been exposed to violence overreact to things, often interpreting neutral stimuli as threatening. Their habitual hyperarousal makes paying attention to classroom activities difficult. These children are always downshifting into a survival mode.

The presenter said the good news is that researchers are finding new ways to train children to control an overactive fear response. For example, researchers have learned that teaching children how to do deep breathing and visualization can really help.

I thought hyperarousal might be part of Mark's problem, so I decided to teach the entire class how to use visualization. I have a collection of soothing pictures that we keep in a special folder. Each morning a different child picks out a picture of a relaxing, soothing place, like the beach. I hang up the picture and encourage the children to look at it often and to try to visualize it in their minds. When I see someone getting stressed, I say, "Let's close our eyes and go to the beach for a minute." Then we stop, close our eyes, and visualize the picture. Mark likes doing this. It seems to help him stay calm enough to focus on what he is doing in class.

What You Can Do

- Design lessons that include movement and interactions with peers.

- Encourage children to participate in intense physical activities such as running, climbing, dancing, and so forth. Exercise helps "kick start" the attending systems of people who require more stimulation to be ready to learn.

- Take time before introducing content to make an emotional connection with students. Remind them of the things that are going well. Then tell them they need to listen very closely to the content of what you are about to say. Ask several children to retell the directions to make sure everyone understands them.

- Always pair oral directions with written ones. Never assume that children can act on what you have told them to do.

- Use pictures of you and your students doing cooperative, positive things together as a reminder of the positive nature of your relationship with them. Refer to the photos often, recalling with your students things you have accomplished or enjoyed together. (Ensure that parents returned the permission to photograph slips included the packets sent to them at the beginning of the school year.)

- Provide children with precise feedback on what they can do to improve their performance. Avoid using phrases such as "good work" that do not specify what parts of the performance make it good.

- Provide children with opportunities to submit several drafts of papers or projects so that editing or making changes is seen as part of the process rather than an evaluation.

- Help children learn how to distinguish between actual danger in their environment and "false positives" (events that trigger downshifting but are in fact benign) by giving them opportunities throughout the day to reflect on their current experience and evaluate what is happening before acting (Sylwester, 1999).

- Incorporate stress management techniques into classroom activities and routines. These techniques might include deep breathing, stretching exercises, yoga movements, affirmations, and calming mantras.

- Monitor the pace of the classroom day to ensure that children have adequate time to make transitions. Avoid rushing children or placing too many demands on them at one time. This can lead to neurological "flooding" and a downshifting to survival mode.

- Remind children several times a day that they are safe in school. Work with them to develop safety plans that include knowing what to do in an emergency and how to respond to peers who may be speaking or acting in a way that is threatening or harmful to their emotional safety.

- Follow through on things that you tell children you will do. Do not make promises you cannot keep.
- Appoint children to a classroom safety committee that is responsible for ensuring that safety rules—such as no running, no hitting, and no bullying—are enforced. Have members of this committee bring up safety concerns at classroom meetings so that all students can work together to solve them.

IMPACT ON REFLECTION

What You Know	You know that children's ability to reflect on what they are doing allows them to set and achieve goals, as well as manage their emotions and behavior.
What's New	Exposure to violence changes the architecture and chemistry of children's brains in ways that inhibit development of self-reflective behaviors.

Self-reflection is an important part of learning. It affects children's ability to regulate their attention, emotions, and behavior. Reflection is considered by some to be an effective deterrent to school violence (Ratey, 2001). Others have suggested that reflection be added as "fourth *R*" to the requisite skills of reading, writing, and arithmetic (Siegel, 2007). Reflection involves receptivity, or the capacity for representational thought; observation of one's own conscious, goal-oriented behaviors; and mindfulness of one's mental state or habitual ways of thinking and feeling. Together, these skills allow children to delay a response long enough to process what is happening, rather than acting on impulse or emotion (Ratey, 2001).

I think Mark is so used to being on his own and making decisions by himself that he has a hard time taking in new information or changing his mind about things. He doesn't really think but, rather, reacts to things. And the reactions are often so emotionally charged that they can lead to all sorts of conflict. He takes everything so personally and has a hard time stepping back and checking the facts before he forms an opinion. I am working with the school psychologist to develop strategies to help Mark be more reflective and avoid the trouble he gets himself into when he acts impulsively.

Receptivity/Representational Thought

Receptivity is the reflective quality that develops within the context of a child's early relationship with parents or primary attachment figures. It involves perspective taking, as well as the ability to process signals about what other people are thinking or feeling. When caregivers are able to develop a reciprocal dialogue with children, freely exchanging thoughts and feelings, children acquire an understanding of mental states in themselves and others. They learn to include representations of the thoughts and feelings of others in their own thinking and come to understand that others do likewise. This allows children to anticipate other people's behavior and understand how these people are thinking, thereby improving the ability to comprehend text and negotiate social situations (Blair, 2002).

Children exposed to violence and other forms of relational trauma often have little opportunity to develop this type of representational thinking. Disruptive or even terrorizing communications with caregivers impair children's understanding of mental states (Fonagy & Target, 1998). For instance, because they lack an understanding of object permanence, they cannot conceptualize that a person or object still exists when it is hidden from sight or that they themselves exist in the minds of others (Craig, 2001; van der Kolk, 2005). As a result, the ability to notice or think about other people's points of view is diminished. These children have difficulty generating alternatives to their own limited perspectives and are seldom capable of seeking alternatives from others. They need help with expanding their private logic to include new ideas. A classroom environment that encourages children to approach problems logically and explore alternative perspectives and solutions provides a safe venue for children to develop the receptivity they need to use reflection as a tool for self-regulation.

The school psychologist suggested a game we could play to improve Mark's ability to separate facts from his often emotionally formed opinions. I use it as part of my reading and social studies lessons. I ask the children to generate a list of beliefs they have about a story we are about to read or a topic we are about to study. For example, when introducing a unit on the ocean, I have them tell me things that they think are true, such as "I believe the water is really cold" and "I believe you can drink the water."

We revise the list several times during the unit, documenting the beliefs that are true and refuting those that are not. I think this is helping Mark see that his opinions and beliefs are not always accurate and that with new information, they can change. I'm hoping this will give Mark the freedom he needs to change some negative beliefs he holds about himself. He would be so much happier if he could.

What You Can Do

- Provide forced-choice options for children to use when responding to questions such as "How do I feel about that?" or "What's my point of view?" The use of the forced-choice format creates a safety net for traumatized children who may be afraid to answer either of these questions without known parameters of what you view as acceptable responses.
- Teach children how to evaluate beliefs by reading editorials, identifying the writer's point of view, and comparing it with their own. Encourage children to research facts that support their position.
- Teach children to think critically about television commercials and other advertisements. Encourage them to check for exaggerated claims or examples of magical thinking.
- Teach children about distortions in art and media that change what people see in ways that also change the meaning of the event.

Ms. Bunting teaches seventh grade in a suburban school. She is worn out from trying to resolve conflicts between the children in her classroom, and she is concerned that she is spending too much time dealing with their fighting. What suggestions would you give Ms. Bunting?

a   Limit opportunities for children to talk to one another. Give them their work in individual folders, then spend instructional time working one to one with them, letting them work on the computer or do seat work at their desk. This should help students avoid getting into disagreements with one another.

b   Provide opportunities for children to learn how to share ideas with one another in an open and respectful manner. Model language they can use to check for understanding. Use academic instruction to train children how to distinguish between facts and opinions or beliefs.

c   Use 10 minutes at the beginning of each class to air issues and resolve conflicts that children bring into class with them. This helps them focus more clearly on academic instruction during the rest of the class.

The correct answer is (b). Children who are involved in frequent conflict with peers often lack an understanding of how to resolve conflicting points of view or negotiate a shared meaning of experience. They need opportunities for direct instruction and practice in negotiating disagreements in somewhat neutral situations before they are able to use these skills to resolve emotional disagreements. Isolating children and providing them with individualized instruction (a) can have some short-term benefits, but this approach does not provide them with opportunities to learn the skills they need. Using class time to resolve conflicts (c) could be effective with children who already have good negotiating and problem-solving skills, but this may escalate conflict among those who do not.

Self-Observation

To a large extent children's capacity to observe and regulate the quality their thoughts, interactions, and behavior determines the quality of their lives. It allows control over their attention rather than leading them to react impulsively to events around them (Levine,

2002b; Siegel, 2007). Self-observation comes easily to some children. Their play includes planning ahead and surmounting unexpected consequences through creativity and wit. Blessed with a strong sense of personal agency, they know that they can control or influence much of what happens to them. They learn early how to use prior experiences to solve current problems. They are good monitors of their own behavior, using self-talk or internalized dialogue to delay action or correct reactions before deciding what to do. They are confident children, capable of showing empathy and tolerance to others.

Other children, including many exposed to violence, find self-observation more difficult. They often act without considering the consequences. They are unable to delay reacting to their "feeling state" long enough to consider their options and make an informed choice. Cognitive distortions about self and others limit their receptivity to input from peers and caring adults. Their attention is focused on the behavior of caregivers as potential threats to their safety, which inhibits the development of self-awareness. Anxiety brought on by a persistent state of fear clouds their judgment, making it difficult for them to distinguish between irrational thoughts and meaningful self-talk or internal dialogue (Siegel, 2007). These children are unable to separate who they are from what they think or feel. As a result, they are often caught in habitual, self-defeating patterns of behavior that they are unable to change. They are rejecting of both themselves and other people.

I've found that it is difficult for Mark to hold on to positive feelings about himself. He can be having a really good day, but if one thing goes wrong or he gets corrected for even a minor infraction, he falls apart. He'll say things like "I told you I was no good." He can't hold onto an image of himself as good and competent.

I am using a scrapbook to give Mark concrete representations of himself as competent and in control. We call it his "islands of competency" book (Brooks, 1991). Several times a week, I take pictures of him doing things well. Mark and I put them in the scrapbook with the date and a brief description of what he is doing in the picture. Then on days when he is feeling bad about himself, I pull out the scrapbook and we look at it together. I think it helps Mark keep things in perspective and not get discouraged so easily.

What You Can Do

- Use the metaphor of a camera. Encourage children to use their "viewfinder" to preview the outcome of what they are about to do (Levine, 2002b).
- Teach children how to replace "hot thoughts" with "cool thoughts" (Seligman et al., 1995, p. 242). Hot thoughts are immediate. They encourage children to react impulsively. Cool thoughts come after taking a deep breath. They help children decide on the best way to handle a situation or solve a problem.

Reflexivity/Mindfulness

Reflexivity, or mindfulness, refers to the capacity to replace automatic habitual thinking with an intentional focus. Individuals are trained to take control of their attention. Observing thoughts and emotions with a certain objectivity or adaptive distancing allows them to notice and change the parts of their unconscious explanatory narrative that limit their ability to succeed (Thomas, Chess, Birch, Herzig, & Korn, 1963). By building on their capacity for representational thought, mindfulness allows children to recognize the self as more than merely the thoughts and emotions experienced.

Mindfulness works with the brain's neuroplasticity to create new neural pathways that can reduce the symptoms of trauma. With enough repetition, these new neural pathways can put a cognitive brake on the "fight, flight, or freeze" response by evaluating the situation and determining whether the threat is real. Repeated use of these neural pathways weakens the fear reaction triggered by the amygdala while enhancing a sense of personal control (Siegel, 2007).

Mindfulness training serves as a protective resource for children whose early attachment relationships are marred by violence or emotional trauma. It builds their capacity to question the cognitive distortions that have organized their lives (Wolinsky et al., 1991). It helps them integrate perceptions of themselves that were denied or ignored in their early interactions with caregivers. The possibility of "goodness" is introduced into the narrative of "badness." The possibility of competency is integrated into the narrative of helplessness. The possibility of hope is integrated into the narrative of despair. The children's attention shifts from people and things they cannot control to self-care—the management of their own mental state and behavior.

What You Can Do

- Teach children how to practice mindfulness. Design lessons to include opportunities to practice self-reflection by using journals, conversation, art, or interpretive movement.
- End each class with a reflective activity that asks children to summarize what they have learned and how it can be applied somewhere in their lives. The format of this activity can vary; for example, you can use journals or class discussions.
- Give children repeated opportunities to tell their stories through writing, art, and movement such as interpretive dance and sculpting. Keep print or taped copies of these narratives, reviewing them frequently for changes in perspective.
- Listen for core indicators of children's explanatory narrative. Encourage children to use their imaginations to change their stories, creating new opportunities for happiness, independence, and success.

CONCLUSION

Exposure to violence changes how children learn and how they think about learning. Traumatized children need learning experiences that foster competence and improve their sense of personal agency, thereby changing their explanatory narrative. They need classrooms that recognize their intense need for safety in addition to providing tools to manage stress and allow the children to stay calm enough to learn. They need to bring their attention under their control through direct instruction in how to train their brain to reflect.

3

How Family Violence Influences Children's Language and Memory

Language involves a variety of complex processes that determine children's ability to interact with others, as well as to encode, store, and retrieve memories. Children use language to engage socially, to organize thoughts, and to process information. Language helps integrate new information into existing knowledge. This chapter explores how exposure to violence interferes with the development of social communication, social cognition skills, and the ability to use language and memory for learning.

Emma's mom and dad are pretty well known in the neighborhood. He drinks a lot and has trouble holding down a job. Rumor has it that mom has tried to leave him several times because he hits her when he's drunk and threatens to hurt the children. Although neither Emma nor her sister have ever come to school with bruises or injuries that would require us to report the family to child and protective services, Emma's behavior in school suggests that she's in trouble a lot at home and possibly maltreated.

The other children don't seem very comfortable around Emma. I think they are confused by how quiet she is. She never laughs and often seems in her own world. I try to get her involved, asking her to help me get an activity set up or encouraging her to join in a game or project, but for the most part she ignores me.

IMPACT ON THE
SOCIAL ASPECTS OF LANGUAGE

What You Know	You know that children's environments influence their communication style. Language-rich environments give children the vocabulary and discourse style they need to communicate effectively with teachers and peers.
What's New	Families characterized by violence and trauma often use a more gesture-oriented communication style. Limited conversation and unpredictable routines can result in a discourse style that interferes with children's ability to communicate effectively.

The social communication skills involved in language development include the ability to express thoughts and feelings, as well as to exchange information and convey meaning. These skills are learned within the conversational style of the home and form the basis for children's interactions with adults and peers. Initially parents and other primary caregivers use their own language to label and interpret events for the young children in their care. In doing so, they shape children's first assumptions about themselves and the world around them. Parents create environments that either nourish or impede their children's language development.

I try to listen to the children when they are playing with their dolls or action figures to get some idea of the kind of language they are exposed to at home. Some children's play involves elaborate discussions of how a doll is feeling or what adventure an action figure is currently involved in. Others, like Emma, only speak to give directions or reprimand the doll for something it did wrong. There is no elaboration or expansion of ideas. This kind of play suggests that conversations at home are limited to information exchange or directives rather than lengthy discussions about what is going on in the child's life.

Caregivers create nourishing environments when they use language that models and encourages the sharing and interpretation of ideas, thoughts, and feelings. For example, when teaching a child how to approach the family dog, a parent may say, "Here comes Daisy. She wants to say hello. Give her a little pat." They let the child know that Daisy is safe and indicate an appropriate way to interact with the dog. Repeated opportunities for this kind of dialogue teach children that language is used to express thoughts, needs, and feelings, as well as to interpret and label events as they happen.

Language-rich family environments provide children with opportunities to develop the vocabulary they need for using language to organize their experiences and mediate their emotions. When language is used to label the steps in everyday routines, children acquire "procedural self talk." This is a self-monitoring strategy that helps an individual assess what needs to be done and initiate behaviors toward a goal (Payne, 1996, p. 92). When children are exposed to this strategy, conversational style takes on the characteristics of school discourse: Children know how to get right to the point and focus on the information being conveyed to them. They learn to use language to tell stories and place events in sequence—as happening in the past, present, or future. Children who live in these supportive, language-rich environments quickly develop the capacity to use language to convey information and to communicate their needs to others. They enter school ready to learn.

Use of Language in the Family

Children exposed to violence often live within families that have a more instrumental understanding of language. In these families, language is used to give directions or control children's behavior. Gestures are used in place of words to convey feelings and relationships. Children in these families have less experience using language to converse with parents and other family members. Their instrumental view of language does not extend to include discussions of feelings and needs. Discussions about abstract concepts are infrequent, as the family's attention is focused more on defining the power relationships among members than on elaborating on ideas or creating shared meaning. When conversations do occur, they are often emotionally charged and somewhat random in structure. The result is a roundabout discourse style, with the story parts ordered by emotional intensity rather than procedural sequence (Payne, 1996). Combined with a limited vocabulary, this lack of exposure to a more sequential discourse style makes it difficult for these children to tell a coherent story or engage in social conversation. In turn, interpretation of school language is laborious, and these children enter school ill equipped to attend to instruction in language-based classrooms.

Social Cognition

Closely related to the impact of violence on children's conversational ability and discourse style is the effect violence has on children's ability to arrive at an accurate interpretation of social events and expectations (Ratey, 2001). Although children who have experienced violence tend to minimize their ability to affect things around them, they also cling to the belief that *they* cause their parents' behavior toward them. They are somewhat pessimistic and tend to assume the worst in any situation. This logic causes them to behave in ways that frequently aggravate teachers and peers (Brendtro, Ness, & Mitchell, 2001). In addition, they are unable to accurately interpret social events and expectations. For example, they may interpret invitations to participate in games or conversations as threats. Because they have limited opportunities for play, these children have a hard time taking the role of the other or appreciating another person's point of view. As a result, they may behave in an impulsive, thoughtless manner that other children construe as rejecting or hostile.

Further exacerbating these problems is the fact that early experiences with violence interfere with the brain's capacity to use language to mediate experience. In typical development, ongoing communication across the left and right hemispheres of the brain facilitates the integration of the emotional perceptions of the right hemisphere with the more verbal perceptions of the left (Hart, 1998; see also Chapter 5). Trauma changes the chemistry of the brain in ways that inhibit the mediating influence of the left hemisphere to distinguish between real and imagined danger (Perry, 2006; Schore, 1994; Stein & Kendall, 2004; Teicher, 2002). As a result children are less able to use language to control their fear response, making it more difficult for them to correctly perceive and interpret events around them.

The other children have a hard time getting along with Emma. I think it is because she is always blaming them for behaving in ways that cause her to get in trouble. She really doesn't know how to join in other children's play. Instead of asking to join in, she grabs the toy and runs off with it or disrupts the game somehow. The school psychologist has been working with the other children to help them understand that when Emma acts this way, all she really wants is to be a part of what is going on. She tells them what to say when Emma grabs something that belongs to them. Sometimes she plays a game with Emma and invites other children to join them. This gives the psychologist a chance to model strategies classmates can use to help Emma stay involved.

What You Can Do

- Provide children with opportunities for self-expression that do not require the use of language. These may include drawing, painting, dancing, and drumming or playing other musical instruments.
- Provide a safe, comfortable place that children can use when they need to recover from an unexpected change in their environment or routine.
- When a particular child is having a hard time expressing why he or she is upset, give the child an opportunity to calm down, then invite the child to sit with you and explore ways of making change more manageable.
- Wherever possible, anticipate changes in routines and activities. Let children know about them and provide opportunities for them to work with you to get ready for them.

- Help children attach words to the gestures they use to describe things they are doing throughout the day. Make a game of it. For example, when children tell you they are going to wash their hands, have them rub their hands together as if they were washing.
- Play board games that give children opportunities to extend their vocabulary in a relaxed and enjoyable setting.

What Do You Think?

Ms. Myers teaches kindergarten in a community where most of the children get free breakfast and lunch. She is concerned because many of the students seem to have a limited vocabulary; it is difficult for them to come up with two or three sentences on any topic. Ms. Myers wants to improve their language ability but is not sure how to do it. What would you tell her?

a   Encourage children to talk and practice vocabulary in the classroom. Use parodies of familiar songs to teach children vocabulary associated with the different topics that they are studying.

b   Have two or three periods of vocabulary drill and practice each day. Include vocabulary that students will need in different content areas. Have them use the vocabulary they are learning by completing at least one written assignment a day.

c   Teach vocabulary through spelling and decoding. Each day, assign several words that the children need to learn how to spell and use in a sentence. Have them read their sentences out loud during spelling time.

The correct answer is (a). Children with an instrumental language style need a lot of practice experimenting with words and learning how words can be used to build connections between people and things. Although it is important for children to learn the vocabulary used in the content areas (b), instruction should occur in an interactive format with numerous opportunities for the teacher to mediate what children are learning and expand on concepts and ideas that come up in sentence writing. Spelling and decoding skills (c) are important in their own right, but they do not replace the need to teach vocabulary in a way that taps into personal experiences and expands children's understanding of the many ways that language can be used and enjoyed.

IMPACT ON RECEPTIVE LANGUAGE

What You Know	You know that receptive language involves the ability to understand both oral and written communication.
What's New	Exposure to violence affects how children process and comprehend oral and written language.

Language develops through the interaction of receptive and expressive processes that together enable the understanding of words and the ability to use them for communication. Language development involves a constant back and forth between thoughts and words. Initially children learn to use words to describe thoughts; eventually, they learn to think in words (Levine, 2002a).

Emma is teaching me so much about how children process language! She is intensely focused on our relationship and how I feel about her at any given time during the day so she often misses the directions I have just given. Everyone else has made the transition to what they are supposed to do and she's asking, "What are we supposed to do now?" At first, I thought she just wasn't paying attention, but the speech-language pathologist helped me see that Emma was paying attention—just to the wrong part of the communication. So now when I want to give a direction, I clear the air emotionally first. I tell the children I am really happy to be working with them. I remind them of things they are doing well. Then I tell them to focus in on what I want them to do. Once I've given the direction, I ask one of them to summarize what I just said. It really helps. I don't have to keep repeating myself. I can use that time to give Emma and the other children individual attention and support.

Receptive language is closely tied to the ability to focus on the content of communication and respond to it appropriately. By age 10, typically developing children attend to approximately 60% of what is said to them, suggesting that receptive language develops slowly in all children. Children exposed to violence have further difficulty acquiring this skill for several reasons:

- Chronically inconsistent, dangerous interactions with their parents causes these children to focus on the relational messages that they receive nonverbally rather than on content (Craig, 1992). Although this style of communication is initially self-protective, within a school context it limits children's ability to learn new information or share ideas (Streeck-Fischer & van der Kolk, 2000).

- States of heightened arousal or anxiety limit the ability to process abstract language (van der Kolk, 2001). As a result, children exposed to violence have a hard time staying calm enough to learn. Their inability to accurately judge the level of danger in the environment often results in unnecessary activation of the "fight, flight, or freeze" reaction, which makes it difficult for these children to process or respond to classroom language (Groves, 2002; Jensen, 1998b; Levine & Kline, 2007; Perry, 2006).

- Difficulty with perspective taking or inferential comprehension interferes with the ability to interpret what is being said (Hyter et al., 2003). Children exposed to violence often have histories of physical restriction and unrealistic parental expectations that limit opportunities for play and exploration of the environment. Because the children are deprived of these normal childhood experiences, they may be unable to take the role of another or appreciate another's point of view. As a result, finding their way through the increasingly complex world of classroom language becomes a frustrating task for these children, often resulting in problems with behavior and self-regulation (Rogers-Adkinson & Hooper, 2003).

What You Can Do

- Provide children with visual task cards that show each step in a task. The cards may be photographs or line drawings. Children can turn each card over as they complete the step.
- Provide children with frequent opportunities to summarize or restate what you have just said. Some teachers include a "summarizer" as one of the classroom

jobs through which children rotate. It is this child's responsibility to summarize the teacher's directions and explanations.

- Combine instructions into a short block, followed by an opportunity for children to work with their peers to discuss and clarify what has just been said. The Columbia Workshop model recommends a ten-to-two ratio: 10 minutes of instruction followed by 2 minutes of peer discussion. Others recommend pacing instruction by using a formula of 1 minute of instruction for each year of the child's chronological age (Jensen, 1998a). For example, in second grade, teacher instruction occurs in 7–8 minute chunks, followed by opportunities for children to process the information.

- Have children work together in groups to summarize what they have heard, generate questions that stem from the instruction, clarify any misunderstandings, summarize what has been said, and, finally, make predictions about what will be discussed next. This process will improve children's ability to comprehend and retain what they hear (Diamond & Hopson, 1998, p. 281).

What Do You Think?

Ms. Evans teaches in a school near a large Army installation, so many of her students' parents are deployed overseas. She knows that many of the children in her classroom come to school feeling stressed. Some have histories of school failure, whereas others are overwhelmed by their responsibilities outside school. She has read that stress interferes with receptive language. What can Ms. Evans do to help her students?

a   Limit class discussions that require children's participation. They may be too anxious to follow the conversation, and asking them to participate is like putting them on the spot.

b   Use puppets, flannel boards, and other visual props to provide a context for what is being discussed in the classroom. These context cues can help children stay focused on what is said. Context cues may also trigger children's prior knowledge and encourage them to participate more fully.

c   Ask a teaching assistant to review oral directions with the children who do not get them the first time. Teaching assistants can also coach children, making suggestions about what they should say in class discussions.

The correct answer is (b). Context cues help children process what is being discussed while providing them with opportunities to develop expressive language skills. Limiting classroom discussions (a) or encouraging an overreliance on adult cuing (c) fails to address the need for children to learn how to interpret receptive language and respond correctly.

IMPACT ON EXPRESSIVE LANGUAGE

What You Know	You know that expressive language is the ability to translate thoughts and experiences into words.
What's New	Trauma and family violence interfere with children's ability to use language to express themselves and mediate their behavior.

The ability to use words effectively benefits children's learning and social competency in several ways. Expressive language lets children think out loud, thereby allowing them to link new information to what they have already learned and to refine their understanding of concepts and ideas (Levine, 2002a). Expressive language helps children regulate their emotions and behavior. They can use words to self-soothe, as well as to consider the consequences of their behavior. Talking through emotions helps children maintain a spirit of optimism and hope in the face of difficult situations. Expressive language socially promotes connection and friendship. Children with good expressive language skills interact easily with peers, responding to their invitations to play and initiating further contacts. Expressive language is an important resource for problem solving and conflict resolution. The more easily children express their opinions and state their concerns using words, the less likely they are to engage in aggressive, acting-out behaviors (Hyter et al., 2003).

Emma hasn't got much to say. She seldom volunteers an idea or an opinion unless it's to say the child across from her is making her mad or that I am making her mad. It's the same with her writing assignments. Unless I give her a word bank and a starting phrase for each sentence, she just stares at the piece of paper. The other children don't want her to work in their groups because she either does nothing to help or tries to boss everyone else. The speech-language pathologist and I are working together to give Emma some ideas about how to ask another child to play with her. We give her little scripts and encourage her to try them out with us. Lately, I've overheard Emma using one of them to ask another girl to play checkers.

Another idea that the school psychologist suggested is using t-charts to help Emma learn the second-grade routines. T-charts are a cooperative learning strategy. You make a chart and label one side with "Looks Like" and the other with "Sounds Like." Next, you have the children brainstorm examples of what a behavior, such as cooperation, looks like and sounds like. Then, you hang the charts up in the classroom where you can refer back to them. They are a great way to help all of the children practice the behaviors we want them to learn, such as cooperation.

Looks Like	Sounds Like
Children leaning in over a table. Children sharing materials. Children handing things to one another.	"Let me help you with that." "You can use the scissors now." "I'll go get you another piece of paper."

Sample t-chart for cooperation.

Emma still has days when getting involved is hard for her. But I do see some improvement. She's getting more work done and actually seems to enjoy working with one or two other children to read a story or complete a project.

Children exposed to violence are often deprived of a home environment where expressive language is modeled or rewarded. Parents who use corporal punishment rather than reasoning to set limits for their children also spend less time talking to them (Straus, 2006). Lacking opportunities to practice using language for discussing ideas or elaborating on experience, these children *do* things instead of talking. When asked to explain their actions or state their point of view, the children appear "at a loss for words" (van der Kolk, 2001). A significant consequence of this communication style is an inability to convey how they are feeling. They cannot describe what they have endured in ways that adults can understand (Katz, 1997). These children are unable to use self-talk or internal dialogue to self-regulate.

Children exposed to violence also have a hard time using language to process what is happening. Their pragmatic language, or social language function, is impaired, reducing their effectiveness in negotiating with peers. This, coupled with their limited understanding of cause and effect, may make it difficult for them to tolerate frustration, resulting in their giving up or withdrawing. Consequently these children exhibit socially maladaptive behaviors such as outbursts or meltdowns that occur when the cognitive demands of the situation exceed the child's capacity to respond appropriately (Greene, 2001).

What You Can Do

- Encourage children to flex their "verbal muscles" by teaching them how to discuss an area of personal interest for 2–3 minutes (Levine, 2002a, p. 128).
- Encourage children to use graphic organizers to note ideas they are interested in writing or talking about. They can use either pictures or words to record their ideas in the organizers.
- Use brainstorming to generate a list of words that are used to describe a sensation, topic, or idea.
- Read stories with children to discover the words or phrases that authors use to describe ideas or feelings they are trying to express. (See the Resources at the end of this book for suggestions.) Keep a list of these phrases. Encourage children to use them when trying to describe their own ideas or feelings.
- Provide children with words they can use to solve problems and resolve conflicts with peers.
- Teach children to practice thoughtful hesitation. This involves teaching them to recognize decision-making activities and output demands as problems that require attention and the development of an action plan (LaVoie, 2005).

What Do You Think?

Mr. White is worried about Maria, a student in his third-grade class. Maria has serious gaps in her receptive and expressive language that make it difficult for her to participate in classroom activities. When Mr. White tries to read a story to the class, Maria starts to fidget and often tries to distract the children around her. How can Mr. White help Maria focus on the story being read?

a   Have Maria sit up front, all by herself, so that she cannot distract the other children.

b   Give Maria pictures of two or three things that he wants her to listen for in the story. Direct her to raise her hand when she hears the part of the narrative she is listening for and then ask her to summarize this passage for the other children.

c   Reward Maria with a sticker if she can listen to the story without bothering anyone else.

The correct answer is (b). Maria has a problem with processing what she is hearing. Giving her visual prompts of what to listen for can help her stay focused on the events of the story. Using a special seating arrangement (a) may prompt Maria to pay attention, but it still might hard for her to keep track of what is happening in the story. Promising Maria a tangible reward (c) could motivate her to behave, but her listening skills cannot improve by motivation alone. She needs some accommodations for her language processing problems.

IMPACT ON MEMORY

What You Know	You know that memory is an important factor in children's ability to succeed in school. Both emotion and language contribute to children's effective use of memory.
What's New	Implicit memories of earlier trauma can interfere with children's ability to encode, process, and store new information. The chronic stress that results from exposure to violence can further limit children's ability to effectively use memory to learn.

Memory is a complicated process that involves both conscious and unconscious information processing. Our memories tell the story of our lives. Without memory, we have no sense of history or relationship. We cannot learn from our mistakes or take pleasure in our accomplishments.

Emma seems detached from her own life. It is like she doesn't know her own story. She can never tell me something she is proud of. I think she tries so hard to forget the bad things that happen to her that she loses track of the good things as well.

Exposure to violence influences the processes of encoding, storing, interpreting, and retrieving memories in ways that undermine both social and academic success. Socially, children's expectations of themselves and others are initially organized around nonverbal memories of interactions with their parents. Although not remembered *consciously*, these implicit memories influence future behavior by priming children to attend to certain stimuli and ignore others (Levine & Kline, 2007). Academically, the chronic stress brought on by exposure to violence interferes with working memory and the ability to process information accurately; as Levine noted "Active working memory craves peace of mind. Anxiety infects it like a computer virus" (2002a, p. 103). Worries fill up space in the working memory that might otherwise be used to process academic information and prepare it for long-term memory storage.

Encoding Information

The relationship between memory and learning is often described in terms of an information-processing model. This model describes memory function through the categories of sensory, working, and long-term memory. These categories do not represent distinct stages in the process of memory making, but are simply convenient labels to help us understand how the brain encodes, stores, and retrieves information and integrates new information with that previously stored (Wolfe, 2001).

All memories start with sensory input that the brain sorts, discarding what it judges to be irrelevant (Gazzaniga, 1998). The remaining sensory input is quickly organized into perceptual patterns that are interpreted on the basis of prior knowledge and what one expects. The brain constantly scans the environment for stimuli that fit into earlier formed patterns. This process of pattern recognition is an important component of learning. For example, children who have frequent opportunities to discuss ideas and predict outcomes of future events create neural pathways that make it easy for them to recognize and encode patterns. This hypothesis testing forms the higher order thinking that is needed to assimilate academic instruction. As a result, their brains have learned to attend to the critical elements of classroom discussions. Conversely, children whose early language experiences are more limited have a harder time discriminating between important and unimportant stimuli in the learning environment. They miss the point because they attend to irrelevant stimuli. This leads to frustration and an inability to complete tasks in an efficient and independent manner.

Emma's attention wanders a lot. She seems to lack the ability to stay focused on what's important in a situation. Instead, she'll get stuck on some detail that interests or confuses her. She seems to lack strategies for getting to the heart of the matter. Even when she's telling me about something that happened to her on the playground, she'll start with all these emotionally charged details, without ever getting to the main point of what she wanted to say.

What You Can Do

- Teach children to look for and identify patterns in everyday life. Work with the children to chart these patterns. For example, what is the weather pattern for the week? What is the attendance pattern? What is the seating pattern at circle time or story time? Chart these visually and add examples to each pattern as they occur.

- Help children become more aware of their own patterns—for example, when they get hungry or thirsty, which times of the day that they have a lot of energy, and when they prefer to work alone or in a group.

- Use games and puzzles to help children become more aware of internal patterns.

- Encourage children to listen for patterns or themes in music and poetry.

- Use artwork and storybook illustrations to help children discover the patterns of shapes and colors that artists use to direct the reader's focus to what they want you to see.

- Encourage children to use words to describe the patterns in their own pictures and drawings. Have them describe why they chose specific colors or shapes.

What Do You Think?

Ms. Monahan knows that children who are exposed to family violence often have trouble understanding rules. She wonders if this has anything to do with why they cannot find the patterns in math problems or stories they are reading. What would you tell Ms. Monahan?

a   Children do not often generalize information from social to academic problems. They think that rules have to do with behavior and with what they can and cannot do. Patterns have more to do with prediction and estimation.

b   Children who grow up in families where rules change arbitrarily often have trouble understanding the concept of what a rule is. This interferes with their ability to discern the rules governing patterns of relationships in academic areas.

c   Finding underlying patterns of relationships in academic subject areas requires children to really concentrate on what they are doing. That is probably why these children have trouble with this sort of thing.

Ms. Monahan is right—the correct answer is (b). Children who grow up in families in which power and authority are exercised according to the mood of the parent often fail to understand the concept of what a rule is. As a result, they often fail to learn the rules underlying predictable patterns. This problem generalizes into all areas of their lives, including social behavior, which reply (a) addresses. The problem in academic areas is that if these students cannot understand the rule informing the relationship, concentration alone will not help them succeed in academic areas, on which reply (c) focuses.

IMPACT ON STORING INFORMATION

What You Know	You know that for learning to be permanent, it needs to enter either the implicit or explicit storage areas of the brain.
What's New	Trauma causes problems in both the implicit and explicit storage systems. Memories of traumatic events stored in the brain's implicit storage area can cause children to behave in ways that neither they nor their teachers understand. The resulting anxiety can interfere with storage in the explicit system.

For learning to be permanent, it has to enter either the implicit or explicit storage area of the brain. Implicit memory stores priming experiences and skills like walking, eating, driving, and decoding words. Explicit memory stores episodic and semantic memories that involve autobiographical experiences and formal learning.

I teach the children how to break our classroom routines into steps. Then we talk a lot about the physical movements involved in each step. For example, sitting up straight is a physical movement we pair with getting ready to write. Next we go through the physical routines without actually doing the task. It's like a game. It's training them to be aware of the sequence of physical movements their bodies go through to complete different academic tasks. For me it's like driving. Once that sequence is stored, you just do it. You don't have to think about it.

Implicit Memory Storage

Implicit, or nondeclarative, memory is an involuntary system that is active prior to language acquisition. Although it holds information that influences how one thinks, acts, and feels, it holds this information outside *conscious* awareness. Memories of reflexive behaviors and classically conditioned responses, such as getting hungry when smelling pizza or pulling in for a coffee when seeing the Starbuck's logo, are examples of implicit memories. So are skills and habits such as knowing how to swim or where to look for one's car keys. With enough practice, these skills become automatic. We use these memories without thinking about them.

Implicit memory uses procedural, automatic, and emotional neural pathways to enhance retention and increase automaticity. The procedural pathway is sometimes referred to as the "memory muscle" (Sprenger, 1999, p. 81). It relies on physical movement to store information in the cerebellum as rituals or routines. Frequent pairing of new information with motor movement helps children gain access to skills and routines without needing to be consciously aware of what they are doing. This leaves more space available in working memory for tasks requiring higher order thinking. For children exposed to violence, frequent use of movement to enhance memory reduces anxiety and builds a sense of confidence in their ability to "get things right."

Automatic Memory Pathways

Automatic memory pathways are like conditioned reflexes—they trigger associations used to recall information stored in long-term memory. Because music is easily stored in long-term memory, anything paired with it is easily retrievable. This is why one remembers television commercials from childhood. Pairing rote learning tasks or transitions with music is a good example of how to form beneficial automatic memory pathways. When used as a cue, music helps children activate their motor memory and recall the appropriate sequence of behavior without having to think about it.

Self-Definition

The emotional aspects of experience are also stored in implicit memory, often in the form of fragmented sensory perceptions and emotional states (Siegel, 1999). These implicit memories are first formed in infancy when children learn to adapt their behaviors to get their needs met. Through repeated interactions, children "remember" to behave in ways that elicit attention and comfort from their parents. Memories of these first interactions become the guideposts of a child's self-definition and future relationships. They become the unconscious rules that govern behavior, or a lens through which explicit memories are perceived and evaluated. Activation of implicit memories does not result in a sense of remembering per se. Rather, these memories are so closely aligned with a person's self-definition that they are seldom experienced "as anything other than the self" (Cozolino, 2006, p. 227).

If implicit memories are of competence and self-control, then the sense of self is positive, resulting in positive interactions with teachers and peers. By contrast, exposure to violence and other forms of relational trauma give rise to implicit memories of danger and abandonment, distorting children's mental models of self and others. Beset by overwhelming emotions and lacking any sense of control over their environment, these children have great difficulty regulating their affect and behavior. They distort seemingly harmless interactions with adults and peers. Upon entering school, aggressive, noncompliant behaviors that are difficult to manage are often exhibited. Preoccupied with physical and psychological safety, the children vie for power with classroom teachers because they feel safe only when they control what is going on. Often both the child and the teacher are confused. Because implicit memories are nonverbal, the child cannot explain what drives his or her behavior. The child just knows that he or she is "bad" or "evil to the core" (Cozolino, 2002, p. 98).

The silence that characterizes traditional classrooms is an ambiguous stimulus that can heighten the arousal of these children, often giving rise to off-task, acting-out behavior (Cozolino, 2006). These behaviors can be so relentless that they result in criticism or punishment of the children when they desperately need comfort and support. The adults' failure to empathize further exacerbates the children's feelings of hopelessness and essential badness. These children do best in classroom environments where teachers anticipate safety needs and involve children in any changes in expectations or routines.

One of the things I've noticed about Emma is that she can't tolerate too much quiet time. At first I couldn't understand what was happening. Everything would be going along fine, all of the children would be busy doing their own work, when all of a sudden Emma would do something to stir things up. She'd say something to provoke me or one of the children. When I'd try to redirect her, she'd refuse to cooperate. Her behavior would escalate, and it was hard getting things back under control.

When I spoke to the school psychologist about it, she said she wasn't surprised that Emma acted that way when things were quiet in the classroom. Apparently children who are trying to manage intrusive memories of trauma and violence sometimes "dissociate" or move outside their bodies to escape the stress. This sense of separation can be frightening, and they act up as a way of reconnecting with what is going on. The psychologist suggested that I find ways of keeping Emma engaged or interacting, even during the quieter times of the day. So now I invite Emma to sit near me or with one of her friends when we are doing quiet work. This seems to help her relax and stay focused on the here and now.

What You Can Do

- Use rituals that involve music and movement to ease the transition from one activity to another.
- Avoid surprises and spontaneous activities that catch children off guard and leave them unprepared.
- Encourage children to articulate their mental models by using words or projects to demonstrate what they know and how they know it.

- Provide children with frequent opportunities throughout the day to give you feedback on what is going on in the classroom, how they feel they are doing, and what you can do to help them feel more comfortable.

What Do You Think?

Mr. Caden runs a fairly traditional sixth-grade classroom. He likes a quiet classroom, with opportunities for children to work on individual projects. He has noticed, however, that the quieter the classroom, the more disruptive Jonathan becomes. He knows Jonathan has had a hard life and wants to help him succeed. What can Mr. Caden do?

a   Use preferential seating and a reward system to keep Jonathan on task during quiet times. Let him use a study carrel. Give Jonathan a smiley face sticker for every 15 minutes that he is quiet.

b   Children have to learn that you do not always get what you want. Jonathan needs to follow classroom rules for getting work done. Remind him of the rule to work silently. Put a check mark on the board each time he fails to comply. If Jonathan gets three checks, send him to the office to complete his work.

c   Recognize that long periods of quiet can evoke children's implicit memories of violence or abuse. The quiet may be making Jonathan feel anxious or out of control. Consider letting him work quietly with a peer or listen to music to help him stay more focused in the present time.

The correct answer is (c). Long periods of silence in classrooms can trigger implicit memories of rejection or danger that, although outside the Jonathan's consciousness, can increase his anxiety and tendency to act out (Groves, 2002). The stress that results from these unconscious memories will make it difficult for him to use higher order thinking to control his behavior (a) while the use of consequences and threats (b) will only further escalate his behavior.

Explicit Memory Storage

Explicit, or declarative memory, is conscious memory (Squire & Zola-Morgan, 1991). It is a voluntary system, intentionally activated when we use language to form memories of words, facts, and places. Explicit memory allows us to reflect on our experiences and learn from our mistakes. When activated, explicit memories conjure up a sense of remembering. We *explicitly* remember how to solve a problem or change a behavior.

Before the emergence of semantic language, explicit memory is much like an unordered assortment of snapshots—capturing the essence of experiences and linking them into webs of associations but lacking a linear sequence. This type of episodic memory continues throughout life, often helping one retrieve information by remembering where it was learned or by linking it to personal experiences.

It is semantic memory, however, that allows formal learning to occur. Learning depends on semantic memory and its ability to encode information in a linear sequential manner—for example, sequencing what happens in a story or creating a timeline of historic events. Semantic memory builds on prior knowledge and generalizes experiences in increasingly complex ways. It grows out of predictable routines and consistent caregiving, as discussed previously in relation to language development.

When children are exposed to violence or other traumatic experiences, semantic memory is inhibited, which leads to difficulty acquiring academic skills and mastering academic content (Cole et al., 2005). Children raised in households where rules and routines are subject to whim often lack a consist method for finding and interpreting information that allows them to move easily into this more sequential ordering of the world. They often require continued adult mediation to help them order and interpret what they are learning, so it becomes part of a predictable pattern rather than a series of disconnected random events.

Emma never seems to have a plan for how she is going to complete a task. She approaches everything in a kind of random way. She's an unfocused reader, often missing details, and then getting really frustrated when she can't answer a question or draws the wrong conclusion based on insufficient information. Her notetaking is the same way. She writes down ideas that are interesting to her but are often not the point of what a paragraph says or what we are talking about.

One thing that seems to really help her is talking about the concepts that underlie all that we are learning about. We have a concept wall at the back of the room with categories like "Whole to Part Relationship," "Cause and Effect," and "Prediction and Estimation." Every time we come across an example of one of the concepts, regardless of the content area, we record it on an a sticky note and put it in the proper category. I think Emma is beginning to use this activity to replace her random approach to learning with one that is more predictable.

What You Can Do

- Have children write stories or letters summarizing what they have learned on a given topic.
- Use acrostics to help children recall lists of related facts. For example, HOMES is a good way to remember the names of the Great Lakes (Huron, Ontario, Michigan, Erie, Superior) (Morris & Cook, 1978).
- Use concept maps to recall important details of a main topic.
- Design instruction so children are given information about the endgame or purpose of the instruction before being asked to learn a lot of apparently unrelated tasks. This type of whole-to-part instruction gives children a context for what is being taught.
- Design lessons so children have opportunities to work with materials in a variety of ways—for example, reading about the topic, talking about it, and acting out what they have learned. This multisensory approach allows new information to be stored in several different neural pathways, increasing the likelihood that it will be remembered.

Integrating Memory Systems

Learning requires the integration of information stored in both the implicit and explicit memory systems. This allows children to unconsciously use rote memory while consciously carrying on other brain functions, as for example when they use decoding skills to read and interpret text. Traditionally, most teachers have relied on instructional designs that require children to encode, store, and retrieve information using only semantic memory. Children are required to attend to verbal instruction delivered in a whole group format and demonstrate what they have learned through performance on tests or other paper and pencil tasks. This instructional model uses repetition and rote rehearsal to help children learn. By design, it strains the capacity of short-term or working memory to retain information, as this memory system has limited space and retains information for only short periods of time. Repetition alone does not guarantee storage in long-term memory; in order for this to happen, the brain also must be able to *consciously* work with and make meaning of the new information while integrating it with prior knowledge (Levine, 2002a).

Instruction that relies solely on semantic memory is ineffective with at-risk groups of children, including children raised in poverty (Payne, 1996) and children with learning disabilities (Bauer, 1987; Swanson, 1988). Children exposed to violence also struggle in this type of traditional classroom. This is due in part to their language and sequencing problems and in part to the silence and lack of meaningful experiences that often characterize these classrooms. Traumatized children are more successful when instruction is designed in a manner that encourages storing new information in multiple neural pathways, using as many modalities as possible. This includes the use of high interest materials, as well as opportunities to apply what is being learned to meaningful, real-life experiences.

Emma avoids doing things that don't interest her. She pretends she's sleeping or doodles on her notebook. But give her something to read or a project to complete that means something to her and she's like a different person. I put her in charge of a class project: making holiday cards for each resident of the assisted living facility down the street. Emma's job included doing an inventory of the materials, sorting the cards by name and apartment number, and making sure all of the names and addresses were spelled correctly. She handled herself so well—didn't miss a detail and actually seemed proud of what she was able to achieve.

IMPACT ON RETRIEVING MEMORIES

What You Know	You know that the ability to retrieve previously learned skills and information helps children continue to learn and succeed academically.
What's New	Exposure to violence can interfere with both recall and recognition, the two processes responsible for retrieval of long-term memories.

Success in school requires children to use both implicit and explicit memory to learn skills and to retain an enormous amount of information. Efficient learning requires that skill sets—such as decoding, letter formation, and the spelling of commonly used words—be practiced to the point of automaticity (Levine, 2002a). This means that they are performed without conscious thought so that attention is given to understanding and interpreting what is being taught. Retrieving knowledge stored in long-term memory and using it to learn new information occurs through two primary channels: recall and recognition.

I am really worried about Emma's inability to remember things she's learned. She seems to grasp things in class but can't translate what she knows into good grades or assignments. I think this is due in part to all of her responsibilities at home. She has no time for homework or studying outside class. It must be so frustrating for her. I need to find a better way for her to retain what she's learned and use it more efficiently.

Recall

Recall is the ability to retrieve a skill or fact on demand. Articulating previously learned historical facts or responding to test items for which there is only one correct answer depends on retrieval ability. Although recall is improved by using instructional strategies that make information more meaningful and relevant to the learner, it always requires a willingness to study and commit a vast amount of information to memory (Levine, 2002a). Recall is highly susceptible to anxiety, a physical problem that triggers the stress response and thereby limits children's ability to retrieve precise, accurate information. Distractibility and low tolerance for frustration, as well as family responsibilities that exceed the children's developmental capacity, often make it difficult for children living with family violence to commit the time and concentration required to easily recall curriculum-related information.

Recognition

Recognition alerts children to the "big ideas" or underlying themes of instruction that are similar to what they learned about in the past. Once they recognize the pattern, they apply previously successful strategies to learn new information or solve current problems. Recognition depends on the ability to discriminate between essential and nonessential information. As noted previously in this chapter, children living with family violence often have difficulty recognizing patterns. Their distractibility, as well as their tendency to "become excessively physiologically aroused when faced with novel information," (Streek-Fischer & van der Kolk, 2000, p. 912) limits their ability to use this retrieval strategy.

The school psychologist keeps reminding me that Emma has a hard time recognizing the underlying patterns or themes that run throughout the curriculum. The psychologist says that this is partly because Emma hasn't had a lot of predictability at home, and she can't distinguish between what's important and what's not. She treats every assignment as some-

thing brand new, even when we've done it many times before. The psychologist suggested helping Emma find the hidden pattern by playing a kind of "Where's Waldo?" game with her. That's helping Emma get better at recognizing the main idea in a paragraph. On some days, she's even able to tell me what operation she needs to use to solve a problem in math! We're getting there.

Promoting Retrieval

Children exposed to violence are most successful at retrieving skills and information that have become automatic. They therefore benefit from instruction that links music, movement, and a positive emotional tone to new learning.

Although emotional memories can cause a neural hijacking when fragments of negative emotional memories activate the "fight, flight, or freeze" response in the absence of any real danger (Goleman, 1995), they are also used to create a positive learning experience. Creating a classroom climate that is emotionally safe helps children remember what they are learning. Learning experiences linked to positive, nurturing interactions with adults or peers strengthens children's explicit memory, making it easier for their brains to encode and retrieve information (Cahill, 2000). Pairing learning experiences with pleasant emotional experiences increases what gets stored in long-term memory by freeing up space in the working memory previously occupied by anxiety and worries about safety (Levine, 2002a).

I try to pay close attention to the emotional tone in my classroom. I try to make the classroom seem as safe as possible, offering Emma and the other children opportunities to sit with a friend or work with a stuffed animal if that makes them more comfortable. I make sure to tell children what I like about how they are helping another child or how they are taking such good care of themselves by eating the right foods or getting their homework done on time. I let them see that they are important to me, that I respect them, and that I expect them to respect one another.

What You Can Do

- Have children write songs or raps to summarize what they know about a topic.
- Use celebrations to link information to positive feelings or emotions. For example, if you are teaching a unit on U.S. history, celebrate important landmarks such as Memorial Day.
- Use simulations, role plays, or physical movement to act out the concepts or skills being learned.
- Engage children in real-life problem solving. For example, a group of middle school children were surprised to learn that a friend of theirs who uses a wheel-chair could not get in and out of the dressing rooms at their favorite store. They successfully organized a petition to make the dressing area more accessible. Surely they will remember the emotion involved for a long time.
- Link what is being learned to positive emotions by using music, movement, visual representation, and skits to reinforce important themes and concepts.
- Embed facts children need to recall into musical parodies or jingles. Sing these frequently to help children learn to associate the melody with the information they need to remember.
- Wherever possible, link a motor movement with something you want children to remember.
- Encourage children to make connections between songs or selections of classi-cal music and information they are trying to remember. Play the music they select whenever you are discussing the topic or when they are studying it on their own.
- Use interactive notetaking to ensure easier recall.

What Do You Think?

Mr. Little finds that the children in his fifth-grade have a hard time remembering what they have learned. They can recall random bits of information, but can seldom remember how these relate to one another. As a result, it is difficult for them to make connections between what they are learning. He wants to help them improve their long-term memory, but is not sure how to proceed. What would you tell him?

a   The children probably just need more repetition. Find opportunities each day for drill and practice. Use homework and computer programs to reinforce the concepts you want them to store in long-term memory.

b   Create opportunities for children to make a positive emotional connection to what they are learning. Participation in meaningful, pleasant activities is a great way to increase long-term memory storage.

c   Do not worry about long-term memory storage. Things are changing so rapidly now that as long as children know where to find they information they need, they will be fine.

The correct answer is (b). Linking what children need to know to meaningful experiences and pleasant emotions is the best way to promote long-term memory storage. Repetition alone (a), without opportunities for meaningful application, is not an effective way of getting new information into long-term memory. Although it is true that there is an information explosion going on (c), children become competent as learners when they can use information stored in long-term memory to think and problem solve.

CONCLUSION

Early exposure to violence influences children's functional use of language in ways that impede their ability to learn and remember. Stress and hyperarousal make it difficult for them to attend to the content of instruction. Emotionally charged fragments of implicit memory often sabotage relationships with peers and adults, making it difficult for the children to participate in classroom activities and routines. They need relationships with teachers who are willing to scaffold classroom routines through the use of procedural and automatic memory pathways. They also need a classroom climate that is conducive to the formation of positive emotional memories associated with learning. In the absence of these supports, academic success is outside the reach of these children and the effects of violence will extend into the next generation of learners.

4

The Impact of Family Violence on Relationships

Children exposed to violence have histories of relationship failures that result in a generalized distrust of adults. Consequently, they have difficulty engaging in positive interactions with teachers. This chapter explores the nature of children's early attachment relationships and how these affect their ability to learn and to relate to others in school. Strategies are discussed for creating meaningful relationships with traumatized children and providing them with the safety they need within the classroom.

Charlie has a history of problems that started in preschool and have continued into public school. He has trouble following rules and is often aggressive with peers. He is a hard child to connect with, often rejecting adults who try to befriend him. By the time he entered my fourth-grade class, Charlie had been in and out of a variety of special education programs.

At Christmas time I bought puppets for the children in my classroom. I looked for ones that reminded me of things I liked about each child. I bought this really colorful parrot for Charlie. I picked it for him because he loves to paint using bright primary colors. As soon as he opened it, he went and cut it to pieces in front of the other children and me. I was devastated. I felt hurt and angry at his total rejection of me and my efforts to reach out to him.

THE ATTACHMENT RELATIONSHIP

What You Know	You know that children's early attachments have a great deal of influence on their cognitive ability and learning style.
What's New	Patterns of insecure attachments can interfere with children's development of the social competencies they need to succeed in school.

Children's early attachment experiences are critical to their emotional and social development. A child develops a secure attachment relationship with his or her primary caregiver when the caregiver provides predictable, consistent care. The environment protects the child from external threats and his or her own relentless internal needs. Within this safety, children use the caregiver's support and encouragement to regulate their behavior and get their needs met (Greenspan, 1997; Schore, 1994; Siegel, 1999). The safer children feel, the more interested they become in exploring their environment. Secure in the protection of a caring attachment relationship, they expand their range of interests and their tolerance of new situations (Fosha, 2003).

Charlie seems to lack curiosity. He doesn't show much interest in finding out about the other children or in exploring topics that are new to him. He prefers to do routine tasks and is most relaxed when we are doing very familiar activities. I think it is his way of staying in control: He only does what he already knows how to do.

Patterns of Attachment

Attachment patterns are not characteristics of children but, rather, of the relationship they have with their primary caregivers. It is not the children who are secure, insecure, or disorientated; it is the pattern of interactions they have with the caregiver that can be characterized in this way (Solomon & Siegel, 2003). These early patterns of relationship provide children with a context in which to develop mental models of the self and of what to expect in relationships with others (Bowlby, 1969).

Secure Attachment

High levels of attunement between a child and his or her primary caregiver characterize a secure attachment relationship. A child whose mother or father responds quickly and sensitively to needs learns important things about himself and other people. He learns that he can make things happen. He comes to see himself as both capable and worthy of others' attention and help. He learns to anticipate positive outcomes from his relationships with other people. The more attuned the parent is to the child's early bids for attention, help, and protection, the more secure the child's attachment.

Secure attachment experiences foster the emergence of self-awareness—the adaptive capacity to sense, attend to, and reflect on how one is feeling. A child who is self-aware learns how to behave in ways that help her get what she needs from the adults around her. This provides her with a sense of competency and control that eventually reduces the need for parental reassurance. Able to take care of herself, such a child is free to explore her own interests and develop her own point of view.

Children with secure attachment relationships learn how to recognize and express their emotions. They are in touch with their feelings and, as they mature, develop the skills needed to communicate effectively with others. These are children who can "feel and deal" with the challenges of social interactions (Fosha, 2003, p. 229). By the time they reach school age, these self-aware children are able to adjust to the increased social and academic demands placed on them because they are working from a secure base.

Insecure Attachment

Children whose primary caregivers are not responsive, who ignore cries for attention or help, do not fare as well. Rather than establishing secure "mental models" of themselves as worthy, these children adjust who they are, and what they want, to the mood of the parent—whom they view as unpredictable and, in some cases, dangerous.

The development of self-awareness is compromised within the context of an insecure attachment relationship. Children fail to develop effective strategies for expressing their emotions or getting needs met, leaving them feeling out of control and struggling to survive. Their focus is on finding safety and protection, leaving them with little energy to explore new concepts or learn new skills.

By the time these children reach school age, the persistent expectation of danger gives rise to a constant need for reassurance (Solomon, 2003). They are quick to interpret a teacher's behavior negatively and respond with anger or withdrawal to any sign that their needs might be ignored or denied. The search for safety and protection replaces any interest in exploring new concepts or learning new skills.

One of the first things I noticed about Charlie was how he pushes the limits, trying to see how far he can go before I remind him of how we behave in our classroom. It's almost as if he is trying to make sure I can save him from himself. I think he is really afraid of losing control. How scary that must be!

I try really hard to give him additional support when he is doing something that is difficult for him. If I see that things are starting to fall apart, I check in with him right away. I ask what I can do to help him stay in control. We make a plan. Sometimes he needs a break; other times just knowing I'm on his side gets him back on track. I think it is so important for Charlie to experience himself as capable of self-control.

Avoidant/Resistant Attachment

Chronic lapses in consistent care by parents sometimes result in either avoidant or resistant attachment patterns. Children raised in this environment take on self-protective behaviors that limit their ability to spontaneously interact with others (Ainsworth, Blehar, Waters, & Wall, 1979). In the case of avoidant attachment, children deal with life's challenges in a manner somewhat detached from how they feel. They do what is expected of them in social situations but are slow to disclose what they really think or feel.

A resistant pattern of attachment leaves children at the mercy of their feelings, often quite incapable of dealing with what is expected of them. They move from crisis to crisis, unable to redirect their behavior in more productive ways. They require more reassurance than other children. As a result, they often benefit from the support of a classroom environment where the emotional tone is positive and the expectations are clear.

What You Can Do

- Provide children with as much consistency as possible. In addition to following a consistent schedule, use consistent rituals to begin and end activities, and use consistent language for labeling activities and giving directions.

- Create classroom routines that teach children how to take care of each other and get their own needs met. Some teachers use a buddy system that allows children to request help or support from a list of children who have volunteered to be buddies. Other teachers find having children sign in on a "Today I Need" chart each morning helps build a sense of community and mutual support.

- Get in the habit of asking children what they need to complete an activity or assignment. Provide them with anything they are missing.

- Use children's names frequently both to address them and to label things in the room that belong to them.

- Have a "Competent and Strong" bulletin board where you display pictures of the children in your classroom illustrating their competency in a given area.

- Provide children with opportunities to experience themselves as important contributors to the classroom community.

- Let children know at least once a day how much you like them and how happy you are to be working with them.

What Do You Think?

Ms. Bugiera is troubled by the behavior of several children in her classroom. She can never be sure of how they are going to behave. On some days they can get work done and seem to enjoy playing with the other children. At other times, they get frustrated easily and give up on trying to do their work. They avoid the other children or pick fights with them. She wonders how she can get them on a more even keel. What would you suggest?

a   Start each day with a classroom meeting. Remind children of the various kinds of support systems available for them to use throughout the day. Encourage the children to make their support needs known and make a plan. Check in with students throughout the day to see if the plans are working or if they need to be revised.

b   Use rewards to reinforce on-task behaviors and positive interactions with peers. Ignore the inappropriate behaviors, hoping that the children will see that when they behave in expected ways, they get rewarded with praise and things they like to do.

c   Use a system of rewards and consequences. Reward on-task behaviors and positive interactions with peers. Use consequences to diminish negative behaviors. For example, if a child picks a fight on the playground, take recess away for the next day.

The correct answer is (a). The behaviors of children with insecure attachment histories are often inconsistent. Use classroom structures such as a morning meeting to provide them with frequent opportunities to express their needs appropriately and experience the willingness of others to respond. Reinforcers (b) may not work because many children lack sufficient understanding of cause and effect to benefit from reward systems. They often think the rewards are given out because the teacher is in a good mood. The same is true for a mixture of rewards and consequences (c). Children whose parents set and enforce rules inconsistently tend to believe the making and enforcing of rules are related to adults' mood more than to an effort to ensure appropriate behavior.

Disorganized, Disoriented Attachment

Disorganized, disoriented attachment patterns often occur among children who are maltreated (Lyons-Ruth, Connell, Zoll, & Stahl, 1987) or whose mothers report high levels of intimate partner violence (Steiner, Zeanah, Stuber, Ash, & Angell, 1994). These children have no clear strategy for responding to caregivers. In infancy, they show fear of the caregiver. They do not experience the parent as a haven of safety. Rather, he or she is a source of alarm. As a result, the attachment relationship is characterized by ongoing conflict that often results in intense feelings of anger, fear, and anxiety (Main & Solomon, 1990).

Children exhibiting the effects of disorganized, disoriented attachment are lonely children who can "neither feel nor deal" (Fosha, 2003, p. 229). They are extremely inhibited and may engage in self-destructive behavior. Lacking a supportive relationship in which to regulate overwhelming emotions, they frequently withdraw from interactions with teachers or peers. They may resort to substances or behaviors that "help them avoid the shame of failure, the anger of unjust treatment, and the grief of recurrent loss" (Bloom, 2005, p. 10). When they are able to stay engaged, they often assume a caregiving role within their families, offering a parent emotional support rather than turning to that person for safety and comfort.

Charlie wrote a story once about being in a spaceship orbiting the earth. He was dressed in a blue sweatshirt with a hood. He somehow got ejected from the spaceship and the door slammed shut, but he was tethered to the "mother ship" by a string from the sweatshirt's hood. He was floating in outer space, unable to get back inside but also unable to let go. I think it was a metaphor for Charlie's relationship with his mother. He wants so much to stay attached to her, even though he gets so little of her attention.

The symptoms of disorganized attachment are of particular concern in classrooms. The inability of children to recognize and accept the parameters of adult–child relationships, as well as their inability to manage their needs for attention, make participation in a group setting difficult.

RELATIONSHIP BETWEEN ATTACHMENT AND CHILD DEVELOPMENT

What You Know	You know that children's attachment behavior is shaped by the response of primary caregivers to bids for attention, help, and protection.
What's New	Early exposure to violence can result in attachment patterns that limit children's capacity to join with adults to get their needs met.

Children's ability to develop to their full potential relies to a great extent on the quality of the primary attachment relationship in infancy. The capacity of the attachment figure to maintain the safety of this first relationship has serious implications for future neurological and emotional development. Attachment relationships marred by abuse or neglect negatively influence the early organization of the right hemisphere. This results in a variety of cognitive, emotional, and behavioral problems (Jensen & Cooper, 2002; Schore, 2001). Like other memories of early attachment experience, traumatic memories are stored in a preverbal, experiential manner that make them inaccessible to language (Cook et al., 2007). Although children lack a conscious awareness of the original traumatizing events, the experiential memories remain in deeply rooted feelings of shame, fear, and anger—driving a child's behavior in ways that make him or her feel even more out of control.

One of the speakers at the workshop on trauma-sensitive schools referred to trauma as "living in the body in the absence of rationality" (Lieberman, 2007). She was trying to help us understand how hard it is for children to make meaning of their experiences when they can't use language to label them. It's like having this incredible sense of anger or despair that you can't explain. It affects what you do, but you don't know where it comes from. No wonder these children try to cope by ignoring how they feel or not allowing themselves to feel anything—good or bad.

Right Hemisphere Maturation

Early research on attachment theorized that children's primary attachment relationships directly affect their ability to cope with stress (Bowlby, 1969). Current investigations of neural development confirm what the earlier research suspected. Children's capacity to regulate stress is dependent on repeated successful experiences of coregulation with the parent. Repeated affectionate and attuned interactions between parent and child accelerate the maturation of the right hemisphere, the part of the brain responsible for emotional regulation (Scaer, 2005). This explains the emotional nature of children's cognitive functioning in the first 3 years of life (Fosha, 2003). These early memories are stored in the right hemisphere experientially rather than linguistically. This means that although a child cannot describe his or her early attachment relationships, these experiences determine what the child thinks of him- or herself, as well as what his or her expectations are regarding relationships with other people (Bowlby, 1969).

I worked in child care for a long time before I decided to teach elementary school. I remember my supervisor in the infant room was always telling us how important it was to hold the babies, rock them, and play little games with them. She said this helped them develop cognitively, because emotions and learning are so connected in infancy.

I think of those experiences a lot when I work with Charlie. So much of his learning is caught up in his ability to feel emotionally safe and connected. It's true of the other children as well. They need to know you like them and are on their side. I schedule time to play games with them during recess. I conference with each of them at least once a week, talking about things they are interested in. As a colleague of mine likes to say, "It's not just what you say to children that counts; it's the time you spend with them."

Social Boundaries

Traumatic memories affect the social/emotional boundaries of children. The fear engendered by the caregiver's inability to provide protection puts children on high alert for danger. They defensively exclude any emotions or behaviors that produce adverse reactions in the caregiver. Desperate to maintain or restore a connection with the caregiver, some children compliantly mirror the preferences of the caregiver at any given time. Self-differentiation is dangerous and therefore avoided.

Other children rebel against the withdrawal of the caregiver, fighting for survival in aggressive and self-defeating ways. In either case, the trauma costs children a sense of connection, both to themselves and to others, resulting in overwhelming feelings of "isolation, alienation, and despair" (van der Kolk, 2001). Unable to gain insight into their own behavior, despite repeated efforts, these children often give up—demoralized by their inability to change (Bloom, 2005).

What You Can Do

- Take pictures of yourself and individual children successfully working together. Date each entry and store them in a photo album. Use the album to help children review the history of their relationship with you. Help them notice the ways in which the two of you were able to reconnect and repair disagreements or misunderstandings that occurred between you. (The purpose of using pictures here differs from the one stated in Chapter 2. In Chapter 2, the pictures are used to help a child establish a history of competence. This Chapter 4 strategy involves using pictures of the child and teacher to learn about repair and reconnection within an attachment relationship.)

- Partner with the physical education teacher or school psychologist to use ropes course activities and other physical team-building exercises to give children a physical experience of competence and connection. Talk about how it feels to rely on one another to stay safe and complete the activities together.

- Teach children how to use a cognitive "brake" to determine whether the signals they are getting from their body match what is going on in the environment. Children can learn to use their brains to monitor their physical reactions by using keyword strategies such as SOLD:

  Stop what you are doing.

  Observe how you are feeling.

  Look at whether how you are feeling matches what is going on in the environment.

  Decide how you will behave.

- Lend children an emotional helping hand. Be willing to actively help children manage stressful and distressing situations that are beyond their resources to handle alone (Fosha, 2000).

- Use positive behavior support (PBS) to help children successfully participate in the classroom. In this context, PBS would include consistent use of developmentally appropriate practices, as well as clear transition rituals, frequent opportunities to move around, and the use of a variety of modalities for academic instruction.

- Teach children how to reflect on emotional experiences, both their own and those of others. This can be done through children's literature and through the arts. Children can be taught to describe their emotions using colors, musical chords, or words. Some teachers ask children to record how they are feeling at certain points of the day to help them see how their feelings change and what events or activities make them feel happy, sad, frustrated, and so forth.

- Let children observe how you think about your relationships with other people and how you make efforts to correct misunderstandings. For example, you might say to a classroom paraprofessional, "Ms. Rodriguez, you looked kind of disappointed this morning when I came into the classroom and didn't notice the lovely art supplies you brought in for the children. I am so sorry! My mind was on getting the science projects set up! Thank you so much for being so thoughtful." Observation of this kind of "relationship repair" lets children see that mistakes in relationships can be corrected and do not necessarily involve high stakes or danger.

What Do You Think?

Mr. Charles is the principal of an elementary school located in a large city. He understands that many of the students have histories of exposure to violence or relational trauma. He wants to put programs in place that will reduce their stress and help them succeed in school. What would you suggest?

a   Work with the physical education department to start some intramural sports teams. Team sports help children learn to cooperate with each other to achieve a goal. It will be a great experience for them.

b   Contract with local artists and musicians to train teachers to integrate art, dance, and other types of performance into content area instruction. Include mindfulness training such as yoga, tai chi, and meditation in the school's wellness program.

c   Sponsor some anger management and social skills groups for the children. They will be less stressed out if they can learn to control themselves a little better in social situations.

The correct answer is (b). The right hemisphere of the brain speaks a language of images, sensations, and impressions. Art, music, and mindfulness training can all be helpful in reducing stress by safely processing information stored in this emotional center of the brain. Although sports and aerobic exercise (a) help some children manage stress, others are unable to manage the physical contact and perspective taking required in team sports. Such activities may escalate rather than reduce these children's behaviors. Anger management and social skills training classes (c) do nothing to deal with the underlying stress response that traumatized children are struggling to manage and contain (Levine & Kline, 2007).

IMPACT ON RELATIONSHIPS WITH ADULTS

What You Know	You know that children's relationships with their parents influence the kind of relationships they are able to form with teachers.
What's New	Children traumatized by family violence often have a distrust of adults that makes it difficult for them to interact with teachers.

Forming relationships with teachers is a dilemma for children whose histories include traumatizing experiences with caregivers. They yearn for the attention and concern teachers can give, yet past histories with inconsistent, disinterested, or even dangerous caregivers make the children overreact to perceived slights or differences of opinion (Perry, 2002). They often come from home environments in which power is arbitrarily exercised; therefore, these children may have a hard time accepting rules. They are not comfortable accepting guidance that is in their best interest unless they agree with it. Quick to engage teachers in power struggles, these children lack the ability to reengage after a disrupted interaction (Craig, 1992).

The district recently sponsored a workshop on trauma-sensitive schools. The school psychologist and I attended to see if we could get some ideas that would help me with Charlie. The speaker mentioned that trauma-tized children "grow up but don't develop" (Perry, 2006, p. 37). That really struck me because sometimes Charlie reminds me of my own children when they were toddlers. He overreacts to the slightest change in schedule. He can have a meltdown over a misspelled word or a project that doesn't turn out the way he wants it to. It really helps me to remember that developmentally he is just not where other 9-year-old children are! So instead of challenging him to "rise to the occasion," I use techniques that work with younger children: redirection, distraction, and the assurance that I am there to help him.

It's hard for me to comprehend how scary it must be for Charlie when he has a temper tantrum. I mean, there he is: a big fourth-grade boy crying and thrashing around as if he were 2 years old. And then he is so worn out when it is over. But the tantrums don't happen as often as they used to, and they don't last as long. I think it is because I really try to give Charlie the support he needs to get his emotions under control. I say things to him like, "I know you must be really angry about such and such. What can I do to help you feel better?" Sometimes he is so shut down that I have to use pictures to offer him a choice of things I can do to help. The school psychologist says that the more Charlie knows that I am there to help, the easier it will be for him to stay in control. From what I've seen, I think she's right.

What You Can Do

- Use ongoing assessments and activating activities to design instruction that provides children with opportunities to make choices about how they spend their time. Let the students know that certain things need to be learned on any given day but that are you willing to collaborate with them to determine how this gets done.

- Provide children with opportunities to collaborate with you on the behaviors that are required to complete a certain task. For example, an activity focused on the creation of a group project requires cooperation and sharing. Give the children time to talk about and practice these behaviors before working on the project.

- Provide children with rubrics that give clear examples of what is expected of them. Offer your support in helping the students meet these expectations.

- Provide additional support to specific children during activities or times of the day that you know are particularly difficult for them. This helps avoid power struggles and lets a child who is experiencing difficulty know you are on his or her side.
- Help children know that disruptions in relationships can be repaired. When a child hurts someone's feelings or behaves aggressively toward someone, acknowledge that it was the wrong thing to do and then offer to help the child make amends.

What Do You Think?

Ms. Cheever is confused. She has read that children exposed to violence are fearful, always on the lookout for danger. But when she thinks about several of the children in her classroom who live in dangerous environments, they seem more defiant than afraid. She wants to help them but is worn out by what she experiences as their constant power struggles. What would you tell Ms. Cheever?

a   These children have seen other people get their way by being a bully. Do not tolerate their defiant behavior. Have expectations. Let the children know that the consequences of their negative behaviors include loss of privileges and suspension.

b   See the power struggles for what they are: efforts to get control of a situation that feels unsafe. Make safety the first goal of all classroom activities and routines. Talk about it often. Have rules and expectations that focus on keeping one another safe.

c   You cannot really hold children exposed to violence accountable for their behavior. It is better to avoid confrontations. If the children do not want to do their work, then they do not want to do their work. It is really beyond your control.

The correct answer is (b). Children exposed to violence see the world as a dangerous place. They need constant reminders that teachers can and will keep them safe. They do need to be held accountable for their behavior (c) but in a manner that takes into consideration where the behaviors are coming from and how they can best be addressed. Predictable routines, protection from bullying, and frequent opportunities to experience adults as positive and protective are better ways to help them manage their behavior than a threatening, coercive environment (a).

Traumatized children live in families where the boundaries between adults and children are blurred or unidentified. They have no model of what to expect in teacher–student relationships. Past relationships with adults have made them cautious or even fearful. The ambiguity they feel often plays itself out in an immediate defiance of any adult's authority. Some children who have repeated experiences with capricious and inconsistent adults confront authority out of a need to control new situations. Others do so out of a need to provoke immediate rejection from the adult, thereby aligning the new relationship with other dysfunctional relationships with adults. In either case, a child may anticipate a dangerous situation that threatens the cohesion of his or her developing identity. When faced with such aggressive and hostile behavior, even the most stalwart professional is tempted to withdraw.

Charlie doesn't seem to believe that I can keep him safe. He always needs to take charge and run the show. He is the oldest of three sons. His mother relies heavily on him. Family stories often place him and his mother in parental roles caring for the needs of the "two" children. They share financial worries, as well as private jokes and memories. When Charlie's mother doesn't have a boyfriend in the house, Charlie's behavior in class is bossy but not defiant. When his mother is in a relationship and Charlie is relegated into the sibling system with his brothers, he becomes unbearable in the classroom. He yells at me, refuses to do anything he is told to do, and is aggressive with peers. Charlie's lost role in his home environment creates an urgent need to be in charge at school.

What You Can Do

- Provide direct instruction on the roles that teachers and students play in school. Define your role as a coach or personal trainer committed to helping each child achieve his or her goals.
- Explain that we all play different roles in different places. Acknowledge that some children are not able to play the role of child at home. School is their place to leave grown-up responsibilities at the door and explore new ideas and opportu-

nities. Some teachers even have a ritual "load lightening" at the beginning of each school day: The children take off an imaginary backpack holding their worries and responsibilities and leave it in the "worry lot" until the end of the day.

- Keep your relationships with children warm but neutral. Do not demand emotional attachment from children. Your job is to help them learn to love and comfort themselves. You need to mirror for them what you want them to see in themselves.

THE NEED TO EXPERIENCE CLASSROOMS AS SAFE HAVENS

What You Know	You know that positive relationships with teachers can mitigate the effect of a difficult home.
What's New	Just one relationship with an emotionally available caregiver helps children acquire the resilience they need to overcome the effects of insecure or disorganized attachment.

Classrooms that offer children opportunities for meaningful connections and quality instruction are an invaluable resource in overcoming the effects of violence and trauma. Positive relationships with teachers help children develop the "emotional stick to itiveness" that is at the heart of resiliency (Fonagy, Steele, Steele, Higgitt, & Target, 1994) while quality instruction provides an effective framework for acquiring skills to promote confidence and self-esteem.

When I first started working with Charlie, I thought he would be okay if I just mirrored back to him all the positive things I saw him as capable of doing. But then I realized he couldn't see his own competence. For whatever reason, he couldn't see a clear picture of himself. So I had to dig deeper. I started using strategies I use with younger children to help them learn how to deal with other people. I told him I was going to be his coach. We visualized different ways that interactions with peers or adults could go. We talked about the worst-case scenarios and what would happen if they occurred. Over time, Charlie started spending less time avoiding problems and more time trying to solve them.

Meaningful Connections

Children whose early relationships are marked by attachment failures benefit greatly from relationships with teachers who create opportunities for successful connection. Opportunities to form relationships with adults whose consistency allows the children to reliably predict expectations and outcomes are key. These adults are flexible enough to adjust to the children's changing emotional states and provide additional support as needed. Repeated experiences of this type of interaction help children learn to regulate their emotions and internal states. They then adjust their behavior to meet the demands of the environment. Over time, they learn how to repair any disruption in the relationship, using skills learned through experiences with the teacher.

One of the things I think Charlie is learning in my classroom is that you can fix things that go wrong in a relationship. Just because he has a bad day or I misunderstand something that he is trying to explain to me, it doesn't mean our relationship is over. We just have to find ways to fix the misunderstanding and move on. I think he is so used to getting kicked out of programs that he keeps waiting for me to say, "Enough— you're out of here." I keep telling him I'm in this for the long haul. I plan on teaching him the skills he needs to succeed.

Learning to repair and sustain relationships occurs most easily in classrooms where teachers use their own affective competence to help children gain control of emotions and behavior. These are teachers who are willing to meet students where they are developmentally and help the children acquire the skills they need to behave in an age-appropriate manner. This means a willingness to engage students in "countless repetitions of attunement [mutual cooperation], disruption, and repair" until they are able to demonstrate the decision-making and self-management skills required to move on with their lives (Fosha, 2003, p. 238).

What You Can Do

- Take care of yourself. The more relaxed and rested you are, the better equipped you will be to respond to children and provide them with the support they need.
- Check with students regularly to see how they are feeling. Adjust the level of stimulation in the classroom so they feel safe and connected to what is going on around them.
- Use music and predictable routines throughout the day to reinforce children's developing sense of safety and control. For example, use the same music to signal the beginning of each class or the transition from one academic area to another.
- Create a sense of belonging through rituals that symbolize the relationships that exist among the members of your class. Use classroom mottoes and songs and a special handshake to reinforce the connections.
- Use Social Stories (developed by Carol Gray; see http://www.thegraycenter.org) and role plays to teach children how to repair disruptions in their relationships with others. A Social Story is a collaboration between a child and a caring adult in which they describe a problem the child is having with a teacher or peer. They discuss alternative ways of solving the problem and the decision-making process that they will use to determine their strategy. Once the story has been used to solve the presenting problem, it can be put in the classroom library and referred when similar problems arise in the classroom.

What Do You Think?

Ms. Weete teaches third grade. Several children in her classroom seem unable to get back on track when something goes wrong at recess or in the lunchroom. She is frustrated because these students often lose a lot of instructional time sulking or being mad after one of these incidents. What do you suggest?

a   Tell children that they will need to make up the time they miss. Set a timer to keep track of how long it takes them to return to what the class is doing. Let them know that they will need to make up the time during the next recess.

b   Recognize that children with difficult attachment experiences often do not know how to repair disruptions in relationships. Use role play or Social Stories to teach them ways of resolving conflict or disappointment. Encourage them to use these strategies to resolve day-to-day issues with teachers and peers.

c   Tell the children that the consequence for not being able to get back to work after recess or lunch is that they will lose the opportunity to participate in these activities. Give them two warnings to get back to work. If the students are still uncooperative, tell them they owe you their next free period.

The correct answer is (b). Children with attachment histories marred by violence or relational trauma often do not know how to repair disruptions in relationships. Rather than assuming that they can get back into control without any support or help (a, c), take some time throughout the school day to talk about how people can repair disagreements and become friends again.

Quality Instruction

Quality instruction supports clinical efforts at "cognitive restructuring"—that is, the process of helping children construct manageable explanations of what has happened to them or around them. It involves teaching children how to bring "linear order out of the chaos of daily experience" (Craig, 1992, p. 67), thereby encouraging children to take control when they can rather than fixating on events and people over which they have no power.

When Charlie first came into my class, I wondered how I could really help him. I knew he needed counseling to help him manage things that had happened to him at home. But I wondered what I could do in the classroom. The school psychologist told me that Charlie's seeing her twice a week wasn't enough support for him. He needs someone with him every day who understands what he is working on and who is willing to help him through the hard times. She stressed the importance of "learning to learn" and experiencing academic success for children like Charlie. So I decided to try and make it work. I offer Charlie my encouragement and support as he struggles to regulate his emotions and behavior. I don't let either one of us get discouraged. It's a new challenge every day, but I think Charlie is making progress. I know I am. I am so much more aware of what I can do to give children the confidence they need to succeed.

Classrooms are great places to help children with histories of abuse or relational trauma integrate back "into the mainstream of relational existence" (Fosha, 2003, p. 250). The teacher's presence ensures relational safety, and the structure of classroom activities is a perfect venue for teaching children the language skills necessary for self-monitoring and self-correction. Classroom meetings and discussions of instructional topics help children use language in a manner that builds bridges with others on the basis of mutual understanding. With appropriate adult support, interactions with other children can reduce the loneliness and despair experienced by many traumatized children.

What You Can Do

- Identify and use scripted greetings with children whose history suggests an early exposure to violence. These children may interpret changes in how you greet them as a shift in the relationship that threatens their safety.
- Talk with the children about your responsibility to keep them safe. Establish a school commandment that says, "All children will be safe to learn" (Greene, 2001). Model what safe behavior looks and sounds like.
- Talk about diversity. Create the interdependence that develops in a classroom where children and teachers share their different talents.

- Never shame or embarrass a child through verbal reprimand or negative comments on written work.
- Help children establish the relationship between physical strength and safety by encouraging them to participate in games and activities that are physically challenging.
- Provide children with advanced warnings of any changes in the daily routine. Even if the change is positive, such as the opportunity to go on a field trip, some children exposed to violence may panic at the idea of moving into a different environment with different rules and expectations. Surprises should be avoided at all costs. Help children prepare for these changes by role playing what might happen when the change occurs and talking with them about their concerns and expectations.

CONCLUSION

Children exposed to violence or other forms of relational trauma have difficulty forming satisfying relationships with caring adults. Damaged by the effects of insecure or disorganized patterns of attachment, these children develop behavioral coping mechanisms that trigger negative reactions from both adults and peers. Classroom environments where teachers reinforce safety and provide ongoing support give children the hope they need to survive. Opportunities to form meaningful relationships with teachers can help the children overcome their perception of the world as a dangerous and hostile place.

5

Creating Opportunities for Self-Regulation

Traumatized children require repeated exposure to experiences that build their capacity to shift from merely surviving to learning. This chapter describes how children acquire the skills necessary to monitor their own behavior and regulate their emotions. The key components of self-regulation are discussed, as well as suggestions for helping children improve their ability to adjust their behavior to meet their needs and achieve their goals.

Jasmine is an 8-year-old third grader who shows symptoms of anxiety and depression. She always seems tense and on edge, flitting from one activity to another. I couldn't figure out why she could never get anything done because she seems bright and has good reading skills.

When I brought my concerns to the Response to Intervention (RTI) team, the school psychologist arranged for me to meet with her and Jasmine's father. Jasmine's father said that Jasmine lives with him because he and Jasmine's mother are divorced. Jasmine goes to her mother's house every day after school and stays there until her father picks Jasmine up on his way home from work. Jasmine's mother is remarried, has a new baby girl, and "doesn't want Jasmine any more" (in Jasmine's father's words). Jasmine's father told the psychologist that when Jasmine was 5, she watched her mother try to commit suicide. That was shortly after her brother died of sudden infant death syndrome (SIDS).

IMPACT ON CHILDREN'S
SELF-REGULATION AND STRESS RESPONSE

What You Know	You know that the care and support available from children's primary attachment relationships help them acquire the ability to regulate their emotions and behavior.
What's New	Violence and trauma have adverse effects on the organization of the right hemisphere, making it difficult for children to acquire self-regulation.

Self-regulation is the ability to regulate emotions in a socially appropriate manner. It includes the ability to focus attention, to selectively use strategies to complete cognitive tasks, and to monitor one's own behavior (Blair, 2002; Diamond & Hopson, 1998; Jensen, 1998b). The path to self-regulation begins with a primary attachment figure relationship, usually a parent. A secure caregiver responds promptly, appropriately, and consistently to the child's positive and negative states. These repeated positive interactions help organize the brain's right hemisphere in a manner that allows control of emotions (Scaer, 2005; see also Chapter 3). The comfort and encouragement provided by the caregiver enables the child to see him- or herself as capable of adjusting his or her behavior to meet his or her own needs.

Jasmine is at the mercy of her feelings. She seems unable to control her emotions, often overreacting to comments from the other children or perceived criticism from me. She acts like everyone is out to get her. If she makes a mistake or thinks that I am unhappy with her, she just disconnects. It's really hard to break through to her. She holds onto perceived slights or criticisms much longer than other children do.

Exposure to violence or other relational trauma interrupts the development of this shared control system due to the adverse effects of trauma on the organization of the brain's right hemisphere (Schore, 1994, 2000, 2001). The child is terrorized by the caregiver's inability to protect him or her from harm. This results in an alteration of the neural structures responsible for managing the child's reactions to threat and danger, thus resulting in the hyperarousal described in Chapter 2 (Jensen, 1998b; Perry & Pollard, 1998; Schore, 1994; Teicher et al., 2002). These early experiences interfere with the child's capacity for self-regulation in devastating ways. Persistent hyperarousal makes them overly sensitive to perceptions of threat or danger. In addition, relentless feelings of fear, rage, and shame are embedded within the child's mental model of him- or herself (Lewis, 2003). Together, these experiences leave the child feeling both out of control and uncared for.

What You Can Do

- Provide children with additional support for activities or times of day that are particularly difficult for them. For example, if transition times are difficult, ask the child to help set up the next activity so that by the time it starts, he or she is already used to the idea.

- Provide children with a visual template for how to complete tasks or sequence directions. Use a line drawing or picture to indicate each step. Mayer-Johnson's Boardmaker computer software (http://www.mayer-johnson.com/ProductsList. aspx) provides line drawings for frequently used vocabulary. (See the extended case study in Chapter 2 for a specific example of this approach.)

- Help children identify their window of tolerance for classroom activities. Teach them to ask for a break, using a picture, sign, or words, when they have reached their limit.

- If children are working with more than one adult, be sure that there is consensus about behavioral expectations. Conflicting expectations among caregivers will almost always cause children with poor self-regulation to have a meltdown.

- Use t-charts to specify what expected behaviors look and sound like. For example, friendship looks like children sitting together at lunch or sharing toys. It sounds like "Do you want to play?" and "Do you want to go to the mall after school?" Review t-charts at the beginning of each activity where you expect to see and hear the behaviors (Johnson & Johnson, 1985). (See the extended case study in Chapter 3 for a specific example of this approach.)

- Encourage children to think before acting by using keyword strategies such as STOP:

  Sssssshhhh.

  Think quiet thoughts to calm down.

  Organize a plan.

  Practice your plan.

- Use rehearsal strategies to help children practice the behaviors that they will need in a new situation.

- Use the "social reading" strategy to help children observe what other people do in various social situations. For example, sit with the child during recess and watch a group of children. Together, observe who speaks to whom, how people get attention, and how they take turns. Take notes about what you see. Use the notes to discuss with the child a plan for how to be more successful at recess.

Interpretation of Danger

The impact of trauma on the brain's right hemisphere effects children's ability to self-regulate when it results in an "overreactive stress response system and an underdeveloped cortex"(Stein & Kendall, 2004, p. 10). Because the brain is organized hierarchically, all incoming sensory input first enters the lower parts of the brain and then makes its way up into higher, more complex areas. Along the way, these "waves of neural activity" are matched against previously stored patterns. If the incoming neural activity is associated with a previous threat, the lower brain's stress response system is activated, often before the prefrontal cortex or thinking part of the brain can completely process and interpret the input (Perry, 2006, p. 31).

This is what happens when a memory of trauma (called a trauma trigger) is activated by something in the environment. The child's brain associates the interaction or activity occurring in the present with past traumatic events. This unconscious connection evokes many of the feelings associated with the earlier trauma. The reaction is so intense and immediate that there is no time for the mediating influence of the higher, more complex areas of the brain.

It is amazing how supersensitive Jasmine is. She is always telling me that the child across from her is looking at her funny or asking me why I am looking at her "that way." She can take a neutral comment and turn it into something totally negative. The school psychologist says it's because Jasmine's brain is hardwired to overreact to possible threats in the environment.

What Do You Think?

Ms. Tobin teaches second grade in a suburban school where several of the families have been investigated for child maltreatment. She has read a lot about the effects of trauma on children's ability to control their emotion and has tried to create an emotionally safe environment in her classroom, but some of the children are still having frequent meltdowns. Ms. Tobin wonders why, in spite of all her hard work, these behaviors persist. What would you tell her?

a   You probably need to get more information about why the children are still having meltdowns. Take some time to talk to them and have them tell you what is bothering them. That way you will have the information you need to make accommodations that will help the children feel more secure.

b   Traumatized children sometimes have vehement reactions to things that seem harmless to everyone else in the classroom. Their meltdowns or acting-out behaviors occur because the children are overwhelmed by their internal states. You should avoid escalating a child's behavior when this occurs, focusing instead on keeping the child safe.

c   It sounds like some of the children might need to be referred to special education. Set up a time for the school psychologist to do a functional behavior analysis for each child about whom there is concern. Write behaviors plans for them based on the psychologist's observations. If implementing the behavior plans does not change things, put in a request for further evaluations and possible alternative placements.

The correct answer is (b). When a trauma trigger taps into emotions associated with past trauma, children need time to regain control. The stress associated with the trauma trigger inhibits the ability to talk about their behavior and the motivation behind it (a). These children have no conscious knowledge of the events that are causing the behavior to occur. Although functional behavior analyses and behavior planning (c) may help in creating successful learning environments for these children, using these approaches should be guided by a desire to relieve the children's stress rather than to diagnose pathology. The behaviors of many traumatized children are appropriate, if dysfunctional, responses to the horror of their experiences.

WHEN EMOTIONAL STATES BECOME PERSONALITY TRAITS

What You Know	You know that all children are sometimes afraid or anxious. This is usually a temporary state that passes quickly when the threat is removed.
What's New	Fear and anxiety are so persistent in the lives of traumatized children that these states become defining elements in the children's development.

As discussed earlier, the changes in the organization of the brain's right hemisphere caused by exposure to violence and other forms of relational trauma predispose a child to continually perceive neutral cues and sensations as threats. As a result, the child reacts with fear and anxiety. Over time, this persistent state of threat becomes a defining element of the child's development (Bremner & Narayan, 1998). And because this reaction occurs outside *conscious* awareness, the child is unable to grasp, monitor, or reflect upon the many negative behaviors and dysfunctional interactions that result (Levine & Kline, 2007; Perry, 2006). Rather, the child lives in states of alarm, fear, or terror—all of which influence his or her behavior in important and predictable ways.

- *Alarm:* Children living in a state of alarm are often rather inflexible, making school hard for them. Lacking object permanence, the concept that things continue to exist even though they are out of sight or hearing (Craig, 2001; van der Kolk, 2005; see also Chapter 2), they expend a great energy trying to control what is going on around them. Transitions and changes in classroom routines are particularly stressful, heightening aggression in some children and anxiety in others (Martin & Clements, 2002).

- *Fear:* Children living in fear often become compulsively compliant. These children may be "too good," complying compulsively with adult requests and often assuming a parental role in relation to their teachers and peers. They may also react with exaggerated fear when their classroom routines change or when a favorite teacher is out sick. These children tend to resist trying new things and are particularly anxious during tests or when called on to answer questions in front of classmates.

- *Terror:* Children living in a chronic state of terror often react by behaving aggressively toward adults and other children (Groves, 2002). They may behave in reckless ways that threaten their own safety and the safety of those around them (Bloom, 2005). Oppositional children defy authority and refuse to comply with school rules and regulations. Their defensive posture frequently puts them at great risk of being seen as a perpetrator rather than victim.

It is important to remember that the behaviors traumatized children exhibit are the result of internal states that they do not understand and that they have not yet been taught to regulate. Children's extreme reactions to what may seem to be reasonable adult requests occur because these adult behaviors trigger the feelings that children associate with original traumatic events. The adult in present time triggers a reenactment of past terror that children can neither understand nor explain (Farragher & Yanosy, 2005). Rather than reacting in a manner that further escalates the hostile or immature behavior, it is important to do *whatever it takes* to return the child to a calm, attentive state (Long, 1998; Perry, 2006).

What You Can Do

- Avoid escalating behaviors by asking children to explain their behavior when they appear angry and out of control. Provide them with a safe place to cool down before trying to discuss the behavior or to make a plan for avoiding similar occurrences in the future.
- Develop a daily schedule and stick to it. The schedule should have a simple visual icon for each major event of the day. Try to avoid abrupt changes in the schedule, but address the fact that there will be surprises at times. Some teachers find it helpful to include an icon for break. This can be placed in the schedule at times when something unexpected happens, such as a fire drill or a bus evacuation practice.
- Design lessons that follow the same sequence of steps, with the same label for each step.

- Develop and use a clear transition ritual between activities. As noted previously, music paired with movement works best.

- Prepare children well in advance for unavoidable changes. If you know that you are going to be out, be sure that your plans for a substitute teacher include pictures of you participating in daily classroom routines. Let the substitute know what transition rituals are used in your classroom. Encourage the substitute teacher to talk with the children about your upcoming return. Have some special stuffed animals available for the children to play with to help them get through your absence.

- Provide children with a variety of modalities that they can use to express themselves (e.g., art, music, play).

- Provide safe opportunities to explore the full range of human emotions through role plays, drama, and literature.

What Do You Think?

Ms. Fingerlow is concerned because whenever she is out sick, the behavior of some of the children in her kindergarten class really deteriorates. They fight with one another and can be really rude to the substitute teacher. What can Ms. Fingerlow do to improve this situation?

a   Tell the children that when you need to be out, you rely on them to behave and help the substitute teacher. Assure the students that if you get a good report from the substitute teacher, you will plan a surprise reward when you return to work.

b   Talk to the children about the possibility of your being away from school when you are sick or have to attend a meeting. Whenever possible, let the children know about upcoming absences. Tell them about who the substitute might be, some of the classroom activities that will occur during such absences, and an activity that will occur upon your return.

c   Plan ahead by arranging, for the children who need it, the ability to check in with another trusted adult or to have a reduced workload. Provide increased opportunities for hands-on, relaxing activities. Provide the children with repeated reassurances of your return after absences.

The correct answer is (c). Telling children they are trusted to be good in the teacher's absence (a) can reinforce children's bad image of themselves when they fail to live up to expectations. Although talking about possible absences (b) is all the preparation most children need, it is not enough to assuage the fears of traumatized children.

Loss of a trusted person, even for a day, can trigger all sorts of fears and emotions in children who have histories of family violence and trauma. Work with your principal and school psychologist to have a plan that can be put in place to avoid students' acting-out behaviors. Ask that the substitute teacher be made aware of the PBS system being used in your classroom.

IMPACT ON THE EMERGENT SELF

What You Know	You know that as children acquire a sense of personal agency, they learn to adjust their behavior to achieve their goals.
What's New	When young children are exposed to violence, they have difficulty developing a sense of personal agency or control.

Living with violence or other forms of relational trauma inhibits the cognitive processes through which children develop an awareness of self. In typical development, children have repeated interactions that nurture the establishment of preference and perspective. Over time, they come to understand that they often can affect what goes on around them, and they eventually learn to adjust or regulate their emotional reactions and behavior to meet personal goals. Trauma diminishes children's confidence in their ability to affect the outside world. Feeling hopeless and out of control, these children are ill equipped to manage the academic and social demands of school (Katz, 1997).

Establishing Personal Agency

Good teaching practice includes creating a classroom environment where children have frequent opportunities to establish and express their own preferences and perspectives. Providing numerous activity

choices allows students of all ages and abilities to develop an awareness of the self. Sometimes that self is similar to others and sometimes it is different from others. This process is called establishing
personal agency or self-individuation. For most children, positive
classroom experiences continue the process of self-individuation
begun at home. By contrast, traumatized children often lack a history of repeated opportunities for self-awareness (Miller, 1984).
Their interactions with their parents are likely to discourage them
from making choices and indicating preferences. They come to realize that expressing preferences or opinions sometimes makes their
parents angry or aggressive. So, these children learn not to express a
preference until they can determine whether their parents are in a
good mood.

*One thing that makes me sad about Jasmine is that it's really hard to
get her to tell me anything that she wants to do. She never seems to get
excited about anything we are doing. She keeps her eyes down a lot,
often crossing her arms in front of her and acting kind of bored. You
never get a spontaneous response from her.*

*So what I've started to do is encourage her to make choices about
really small, unimportant things, like what color marker she wants to use
for an art project. Then I keep track of what she chooses. That lets me
give her feedback like, "Jasmine, you must really like blue, because you
always pick the blue marker when we draw." The school psychologist says
this is a safe, nonthreatening way for Jasmine to explore her preferences.
It really doesn't take extra time. I just need to be more focused with
Jasmine than with the other children. And if that's what it takes to help
her become more sure of herself, I am more than willing to do it.*

What Do You Think?

Ms. DiTrano is frustrated by the lack of motivation she observes in many of her fifth-
grade students. She cannot get them to participate in any of the classroom activities.
She has tried consequences and rewards, but nothing seems to work. What would
you suggest?

a   Provide children with a lot of opportunities to tell you about their interests. Use this information to design lessons that address content through the children's interests.

b   Adjust your expectations so that you are not continually discouraged by the children's lack of motivation. Stay focused on helping the children who are willing to work with you.

c   Let parents know that any work not completed in class will be sent home as homework and that if the work is still not completed, the child will receive a failing grade.

The correct answer is (a). Designing lessons based on student preferences and interests is a good way to increase participation. This is especially true for children who lack self-awareness and personal agency. Including their preferences in instructional designs helps them acquire an appropriate sense of control over their environment. Lowering expectation (b) or chastising children for incomplete work (c) only makes them feel less in control.

When children live in families where indications of preference can tip the balance between parental indifference and parental aggression, self-exploration soon gives way to survival. In fact, survival becomes an overriding goal. Distracted from their primary task of self-discovery, these children quickly learn that safety is best achieved through a "sensory muting" that allows them to mirror the preferences of the caregiver (Helfer & Kempe, 1980, p. 69). These survival mechanisms have a profound impact on the development of the self. Curiosity and exploration are replaced with hypervigilance. Spontaneous play gives way to repetitive reenactments of traumatizing events that the child has witnessed or personally experienced.

Every story Jasmine writes is about somebody not liking the main character. Sometimes she'll write about an animal that gets left behind in the nest when the mother takes everyone but her. Or she'll create a world where danger is everywhere, lurking around every corner. Every now and then, she'll have the character take control and find a way out, but usually these stories ends abruptly, with no actual escape from the situation.

The price children pay for sacrificing self-exploration to survival is the inability to define the boundaries of the self and thereby to experience self-control, which in turn gives rise to absence of feeling and a sense of incompetence. This inability to differentiate the self from the environment limits all areas of development. It impairs children's ability to develop a cognitive sense of self independent from the people with whom they interact. Attention is directed outward, as the children try in many ways to become whomever the adults in power want them to be. Self-awareness is replaced with a desire to please others whom they perceive as having power or control in the situation. Repeated focus on pleasing others rather than making decisions based on their own intrinsic self-worth leaves these children at high risk for substance abuse and other forms of dangerous behaviors (Dayton, 2000).

What You Can Do

- Provide children with opportunities throughout the day to make choices. Start with safe, simple things, such as which color paper they want to use or whether they want to sit at their desk or in a quiet area for reading. Once the choice is made, use a simple bar graph to record it and thereby let children keep track of the choices they have made throughout their day.

- End each lesson with an opportunity for children to share what they learned about their topics of interest. Chart the results on an easy-to-read graph so the children can see which choices they have made throughout the day.

- Encourage children to come up with ideas about how to address issues that occur during the day. Examples include "We have a few minutes to go before recess. Can someone come up with a game we could play?" and "It looks like you and Bobby left the art area kind of messy. What can you do to clean it up?" (Doll et al., 1996).

- Use rubrics to help children self-evaluate their performance against a model. For example, "I started each sentence with an uppercase letter just like the rubric."

- Provide each child with a scrapbook. Include pictures showing the student following the rules or helping other children out, as well as work samples that demonstrate competence. Date all of the entries. Meet with each child regularly to review his or her scrapbook, and comment on the child's growing ability to set a goal and achieve it. When a child has a bad day and believes that he or she can do nothing right, use the student's scrapbook to review his or her history of competence and control.

- Encourage children to plan for upcoming activities. If a classroom celebration is coming up, spend time beforehand talking about the related games or music that the children would like the activity to include. If they are going to the library, talk about the kind of books they want to be on the lookout for. Use a visual chart to record the findings.
- Get in the habit of doing several self-referent activities each day. For example, use children's names when addressing them, label children's belongings with their names, and so on.

REGULATING EMOTIONAL STATES

What You Know	You know that emotional regulation includes the ability to label feelings, express them safely, and regulate one's internal reactions so that feelings are not experienced as overwhelming.
What's New	Children exposed to violence often have difficulty differentiating between emotional states. They often lack the ability to use language to describe how they are feeling.

Emotional regulation involves both cognitive and psychological processes. Cognitively, children need the ability to differentiate between feelings and the vocabulary to label them correctly. Psychologically, children must be able to control how they express feelings and how these feelings affect their internal state.

The school psychologist has helped me understand that children as young as Jasmine can have a pretty pessimistic view of life. They hit bottom pretty quickly—reacting to the slightest negative event with a sense of hopelessness and helplessness. The psychologist says we have to help Jasmine learn how to take things in stride and to feel more in control of her reactions to things. Lately, I have noticed that when Jasmine's experiencing difficulties with a situation in the classroom, she recovers faster than she did at the beginning of the year. I hear her using the scripts we've taught her, like "Let it go" and "Don't sweat the small stuff." It makes me happy to see her feeling a little more hopeful.

Children with histories of secure attachment enter school able to flexibly regulate stressful emotional states with the help of feedback from others and their own growing self-regulation. Past experiences with adults have taught them to trust teachers and other caregivers. Consequently, they can comply with adult requests and are easily redirected. They have an accurate internal compass that cues them to adjust their behavior to meet the expectations of the situation.

Children whose early attachment relationships are marred by exposure to violence or other trauma have greater difficulty adjusting to the emotional demands of a situation. Negative past experiences with adults leave emotional scars that make forming new relationships difficult. These children have trouble distinguishing between rules that represent an arbitrary use of power and those that are in their best interest (Cole et al., 2005). As a result, interactions with teachers often trigger overwhelming emotions that the child is unable to control or explain.

What Do You Think?

Mr. O'Callahan teaches fourth grade in a school where family and community violence is quite common. He is shocked by the stories he overhears on the playground about kids getting shot and parents going to jail. He wants to have a good year with his class but is concerned about how to create an environment where children feel safe enough to learn. What would you tell him?

a   Have a set of rules and consequences in place when the children arrive at the beginning of the school year. Let students know that you expect them to follow the rules and that failure to do so will result in two warnings. After the third offense, they will be sent to the principal's office and will be allowed to return to classroom only after there is home–school agreement on a behavior management plan.

b   Recognize that children exposed to violence may not have a clear under-standing of how rules can protect them and keep them safe. Have a class-wide meeting to discuss how to create a safe and caring classroom. Post a list of three to five rules that everyone agrees to follow to keep the class-room safe. Set aside several times during the day when you and the chil-dren can review how things are going and make any changes necessary to keep everyone safe.

c   Do not expect too much. Limit the academic expectations until everyone's behavior is under control. Use a level system of behavior management whereby children need to earn the right to every classroom privilege, including use of materials and permission to speak to other children.

The correct answer is (b). Physical safety is an important priority in schools where many of the children enrolled are exposed to violence. Many children exposed to violence misunderstand the meaning of rules (a) and may lack the self control to follow them without support (c). The best way to help these students learn to control their behav-iors is to create a behavior management system that focuses on maintaining safety while promoting personal agency, team building, self-reflection, and problem solving.

Traumatized children often do not know how they feel (Brendtro, Ness, & Mitchell, 2001). Experiences with inconsistent or abusive caregivers make it difficult for them to differentiate between emotional states. Because their parents' facial expressions are frequently at odds with their words, children have little confi-dence in their own ability to read emotions correctly. There is no stable frame of reference for reading and interpreting the emotional landscape. These deficits, coupled with the powerful emotional reactions brought on by repeated exposure to violence, give rise to feelings that are intense and out of control (Cook et al., 2005).

Children who lack emotional regulation are at significant risk of school failure, since academic success depends to a large extent on children's ability to regulate their emotions. Children's ability to focus their attention, energize their bodies, and organize their thinking in ways that are adaptive to their needs depends on emotional regulation (LeDoux, 2002). Children who lack emotional regulation are often "chronically tense and hyper-aroused with hair-trigger tempers and a compromised ability to manage distressing emotions" (Bloom, 2005, p. 10). Over time, repeated experiences of feeling emotionally overwhelmed cause these children to believe that they are incapable of acquiring the self-control observed in their peers. They give up, unable to reverse the pattern of failure in relationships and learning.

When I first had Jasmine in my classroom I was baffled by her refusal to talk things through with me. With the other children, you give them some time to cool off, and then they will problem-solve with you. Jasmine won't do this. She carries a grudge for days. Refusing to talk. Refusing to move on. The school psychologist encouraged me to give Jasmine a lot of space, to not demand too much interaction with Jasmine but to be fair and kind. I wasn't sure it would work. I wanted Jasmine to feel better, to not be so sad. But, I tried it out. And do you know, she started to come around. I think she needed to know that I wasn't going to put emotional demands on her she couldn't meet.

The first step in helping children learn to regulate their emotions is to make them more aware of how different emotions feel. The next step is to teach them a vocabulary they can use to label feelings as they are experienced. The greater the vocabulary children have available to describe emotions, the easier it becomes for them to more precisely describe exactly how they are feeling. Finally, children need to learn how to tolerate feeling states without fear of losing control. Whereas nonabusive parents can serve as safe havens for their children's emotional reactions, offering them words to label their experiences or safe ways to express what they are feeling and ideas for modulating their reactions, abusive parents cannot. Abusive parents often respond to displays of emotion in ways that teach children that their emotions are scary and destructive. As a result, children learn to avoid feelings, lest they be destroyed by them.

What You Can Do

- Read stories that explore and illustrate the whole range of human emotions. Books can be a great source of information about the kinds of emotions that people experience and safe ways to express them. See the resource list at the end of the book for suggested books.

- Talk with your students about how you are feeling and things you do to help yourself feel happy and in control. For example, you might say to the children, "This weekend our cat died. He was 12 and we had him since he was a kitten. We were all so sad. We cried a little bit and then my husband said, 'Let's make a poster of all the fun things we did with Toby.' So we spent the afternoon finding pictures of us doing fun things with Toby, and we put them on the poster. Then we wrote Toby a note thanking him for being a good pet. We put the poster and the note on the hall table so we could remember Toby and not be so sad." Fred Rogers, of the television show *Mr. Rogers' Neighborhood,* was a master at using this technique, which speech-language pathologists call "sports casting" or "forecasting," to walk children through everyday experiences. When this approach is used to teach children emotional regulation, the children learn to use the vocabulary that describes different emotions and a model for expressing the emotions safely.

- Have students use journaling and other writing activities to help them find the words to describe feeling states. Remind them that they can include feeling words, such as *frustrated, sad, excited, nervous,* and *happy,* on classroom word walls and in other instructional activities.

- Teach children to notice how they feel. Ask them to describe how their bodies feel after engaging in aerobic exercise compared with sitting still for a long time. Call attention to the activities that help them feel good. Chart these and refer back to them when a child is feeling discouraged and needs a boost.

- Teach children how to use their minds to control their emotions and moods. Use techniques such as visualization, deep breathing, or yoga poses to help children be more aware of their physical states.

- Help children set individual goals for each activity block throughout the day. At the end of each period, ask each student if he or she met his or her goals. This combination of goal setting and self-reflection is a powerful way to help children learn to adjust their behaviors to meet their goals. Some teachers use a traffic light to help children evaluate their progress in reaching their goals. A green light signals that the child is on the right track and meeting his or her goal. A yellow light means that the child needs some redirection but is still focused on his or her goal. A red light means that it is time for the child to stop, refocus, and try again. Several times during the day the children and teacher check in with one another. Depending on how the child rates his or her behavior, he or she receives a green, yellow, or red circle next to his or her name.

- Teach children to use scripts or self-talk to manage situations that are particularly difficult for them.

ACQUIRING AGE-APPROPRIATE SOCIAL SKILLS

What You Know	You know that behavioral regulation involves the capacity to correctly "read" social situations and adjust behaviors accordingly. It is dependent on the acquisition of age-appropriate social skills.
What's New	When children are exposed to violence, they are less able to appraise situations accurately and respond to stress appropriately, so they are likely to overreact to perceived threats.

Learning to regulate behavior has profound academic and social consequences for children. Academic success requires children to adjust their behavior to pay attention, complete work in a timely manner, and master material taught in the content areas. Socially, children need to learn how to read social cues and adjust their behaviors to meet the demands of different social situations and to interact with others. School-age children with age-appropriate social skills are likely to be more popular and capable of forming friendships and long-term relationships than their peers are who lack these skills (Oden, 1988).

The other children are a little wary of Jasmine. She is so quick to get angry or accuse them of doing something to get her in trouble. I am concerned that they don't invite her to play or to sit with them at lunch. I am afraid their behavior toward her will reinforce her already negative feelings about herself.

The Arousal Continuum

An important distinction between traumatized children and their peers is that what are viewed as "transitory traits" in most children become "states of being" in traumatized children. For example, many children may show signs of alarm when they hear a loud sound or temporarily lose sight of their parent in a store. Once they are reassured about the noise or reunited with the parent, these children return to a calm/attentive level of arousal, with no permanent changes in their way of interacting with the world. This is not the case for children who are repeatedly exposed to violence and other forms of danger. The circumstances of their lives cause changes in the architecture and chemistry of the brain that do not go away when the danger is removed (Perry, 2006; Schore, 1994; Stein & Kendall, 2004; Teicher, 2002).

Children's ability to regulate their behavior is strongly influenced by changes in their state of arousal. Perry (2006) proposed a five-point continuum of arousal that begins with a state of calm and, with increased perception of threat, rises through attention, alarm, and fear to a state of terror. As children's arousal states change, the area of the brain controlling their thinking and behavior also changes. When a child is calm, thinking and behavior are regulated by the neocortex, the part of the brain that controls higher level thinking processes. The child is able to use higher order thinking skills and self-reflection for problem solving and behavior regulation. As fear escalates, regulating control shifts to the brain's limbic system, or the area that controls emotions. Thinking becomes more reactive, and it is more difficult for the child to control inappropriate, impulsive behaviors.

I attended a workshop where the presenter explained that our arousal state really affects how we act. That's because different parts of the brain regulate thinking and behavior at different levels of arousal. So if I'm nice and calm, I'm able to think clearly and solve problems easily, because the neocortex is in charge. If I'm totally stressed and cranky, I'm more likely to make "mountains out of molehills" and fly off the handle at the slightest thing, because stress causes the limbic system to take over as regulator. That's the part of the brain that signals the fight or flight response. The body goes into a survival mode that makes higher order thinking impossible. That workshop really made me appreciate how important it is for me to maintain a classroom environment where children like Jasmine feel safe and are calm enough to learn.

What Do You Think?

Ms. Sanchez wants her first-grade classroom to be a place where children feel safe and calm enough to learn. She tries to be emotionally available, using proximity and a quiet voice to build children's confidence in their ability to learn. She wonders what else she can do to create a comfortable environment. What would you suggest?

a   Check in with children several times a day, letting them know how you think they are doing in terms of keeping the classroom safe. If they are behaving in an unsafe way, give them suggestions about how to turn their behavior around.

b   Teach children how to let you know where they are on the arousal continuum. Show them how to use pictures or gestures to indicate if they are feeling calm or if they have moved up the continuum to alarm or fear. Check in several times each day, and be willing to adjust what is going on in the classroom based on their feedback.

c   Use tokens or points to reward children's on-task behaviors. Let them know that the more frequently they earn a reward, the more quickly they can cash them in for things they may enjoy. Praise the children who earn the most points or tokens.

The correct answer is (b). An important part of teaching children how to regulate their behavior is to help them recognize changes in their arousal state and make the necessary adjustments to return to a calm/attentive state. Letting them know how you think they are doing does not give them a strategy for checking in on their own internal state and may make them become more aroused if they feel they are being misjudged (a). Rating or rewarding children's behavior for them may increase compliance but not a sense of personal safety (c).

ACQUIRING SELF-SOOTHING SKILLS

What You Know	You know that as children mature, they learn to monitor their own behavior and internal states. They learn to use self-soothing strategies to calm themselves down.
What's New	Children exposed to violence often lack insight into how they are feeling and why. They may lack age-appropriate strategies for self-soothing.

As they grow older, most children acquire strategies they use to feel better when they are stressed. These include self-soothing messages, affirmations, music, and physical activity. Sometimes they talk to a caring adult, trusting that person to support their efforts to problem-solve. These self-soothing strategies help children calm down, relax, and let go of negative emotions before they spill over into problem behaviors. Children who are traumatized by family violence cannot use these strategies as effectively as their peers. This is due in part to their inability to differentiate between feeling states. For example, they may be unable to distinguish between excitement over an upcoming field trip and anxiety over a test. Past negative experiences with attachment figures limit their ability to be comforted by caring adults. It is therefore important to provide these children with opportunities to engage in comforting routines that they initiate on an as-needed basis.

When I found out that Jasmine was going to be in my classroom, I was a little nervous at first. I heard she had a lot of meltdowns. I knew there was nothing I could do to make her feel better when she was in a melt-

down. Her pain was too great. And her trust was too little. She needed to learn to comfort herself. So I made a deal with her. I put several cotton blankets and some stuffed animals in the reading corner, near the rocking chair. I told her that whenever she felt a meltdown coming on, she could curl up in a blanket until she felt better. In the beginning, she'd head right for the rocking chair and blanket as soon as she got off the bus. Sometimes she stayed there for 15–20 minutes. Now she only needs to use the rocking chair for 2–3 minutes before she's back in the thick of things. The rocker and blankets really helped. Jasmine smiles more now and is learning to play with the other children. Every now and then, she even takes my hand on the way to lunch or recess.

What You Can Do

- Create a climate of emotional safety by establishing classroom rules that encourage respect for one another.
- Remind children frequently that you are there to keep them safe.
- Provide children with opportunities to observe how they feel by using some type of rating scale (e.g., *tired, excited, sad, happy*).
- Offer children the opportunity to select activities that help them maintain a comfortable state of arousal (e.g., physical activity, deep breathing, visualization, physical proximity to an adult).

CONCLUSION

Children with histories of exposure to violence or relational trauma often enter school without age-appropriate self-regulatory skills. Teachers play an important role in helping these children learn to monitor and control their emotions and behavior. Classroom activities that promote choice making and self-reflection help children experience themselves as competent and in control. A classroom climate of encouragement and support provides the safe haven that these children need to face the future with confidence and hope.

6

Supporting the Acquisition of Reading and Writing Skills

Childhood trauma can have a detrimental effect on the acquisition of reading and writing skills. This chapter highlights literacy learning practices that are particularly helpful to traumatized children. These include creating a social context for literacy instruction, providing repeated opportunities for teacher-mediated instruction, and creating a trauma-sensitive approach to teaching writing.

Tyrone was on probation when he was assigned to my sixth-grade classroom. He had gotten into a fight with his father, who filed a Child in Need of Supervision (CHINS) petition against him. He was sent to a detention center for a few months and had recently returned home. Tyrone's father had moved out, so Tyrone was living with his mother, grandmother, and two sisters. Tyrone blamed himself for his father leaving the family. He felt bad that his mother was having trouble making ends meet and needed to get a second job. Tyrone was trying to help out where he could, taking care of his sisters and watching out for his grandmother. He was pretty distracted and seemed tired all the time. He told me he was sick of school. He had no friends and the work was boring. All they ever did was phonics; he thought that he was never going to learn how to read. Although he denied it, I think he was ashamed of what he didn't know. He pretended not be by saying that he wanted to quit and get a job.

CREATING A SOCIAL CONTEXT FOR READING INSTRUCTION

What You Know	You know that the home environment influences children's ability to learn how to read and write.
What's New	The emotional tone that surrounds shared reading experiences between parents and children affects children's literacy development.

Learning to read is first and foremost a social practice that for many children begins in the emotional context of shared reading experiences with parents (Axford, 2007). Studies investigating the relationship between attachment and literacy suggest that successful development of emergent literacy skills is contingent on a secure attachment between parent and child (Frosch, Cox, & Goldman, 2001). Through shared reading within a secure and stable environment, parents help children begin to understand how meaning is constructed from print (Tovani, 2000). They teach their children how to approach reading in a systematic way: asking questions about what might happen next and noticing the strategies a character uses to solve a problem or reach a goal. Positive memories of this shared time are an important reminder to children that reading is pleasurable as well as purposeful.

Tyrone avoided reading whenever he could. He was clearly overwhelmed by the complexity of trying to decode words and interpret text. He covered his embarrassment about his poor reading by playing the class clown or complaining about how "stupid" the assignments were. I wondered if I would be able to break through to him and help him out.

Children traumatized by family violence are often deprived of the early literacy experiences enjoyed by other children (Haeseler, 2006). They have fewer opportunities to explore books or participate in shared reading with their parents. Even when reading takes place, the interaction between parent and child is often strained if correction tactics are harsh, and interactions are limited (Bergin, 2001). As a result, these children are denied both the mediating presence of an adult who can show them how to approach text in a purposeful manner and the pleasurable memories usually associated with shared reading.

Reading in School

The lack of a positive early reading experience, coupled with the language and conceptual problems discussed in previous chapters, threatens the ability of children traumatized by violence to approach reading in a thoughtful, strategic way. They require help from teachers to build confidence in their ability to read, as well as to develop strategies to address text in a purposeful manner.

The physical environment plays an important role in establishing the trust and safety children need to collaborate with teachers to make meaning from text. Comfortable spaces should be provided where children can read to and read with one another, as well as in small groups or individually with the teacher.

The emotional climate of the classroom should foster a relaxed, enjoyable discussion of favorite books. Shared reading, as well opportunities to write alternative endings to stories or change the setting or attributes of the main characters, should occur frequently. These activities help children approach reading in a creative, playful manner that can assist them in overcoming any anxiety they may feel about learning how to read.

I think emotional safety is perhaps the most important part of teaching reading to children who struggle to connect with and make meaning from text. The physical environment is a really important part of helping children to feel safe. The reading area in my room has a cozy feeling to it. I have two couches there and several beanbag chairs. I encourage children to read together there, either to one another or just sitting side by side. I think that gives them more confidence than reading alone, and they can talk about the text with one another.

And we talk about books all the time! I have multiple versions of a lot of traditional children's stories. We spend a lot of time comparing and contrasting how different authors handle different plot points or discussing the attributes of the main characters. I help the children understand that these differences sometimes reflect the author's culture. For example I tell them about "Cinderfella" the Irish version of the Cinderella story told from a boy's point of view. Sometimes we all rewrite a section of a text we are working on, giving it a personal and sometimes surprising twist. Then we read what we have written to one another. It's a lot of fun, and I think it builds the children's confidence.

What You Can Do

- Provide children with numerous opportunities to explore the context of the stories they are going to be reading. For example, if the students are going to be reading about the Old West, provide opportunities for them to learn some of the music that was sung during that period. Bring in food or tools that are similar to those described in the text.

- Read stories to children that are about the town where they live or about the natural habitat around them. Teach them to use books to find out more about the birds and animals that are in their environment. This helps children who are living in difficult home situations realize that they are part of a larger, gentler world.

- Read stories about people who overcome great adversity to go on and make an important contribution to their communities.

- Integrate characters from favorite books into problems children are trying to solve in the classroom. Have discussions about what they think their favorite character might do and why.

- As you get to know individual students, find books that remind you of their best qualities and attributes. Share these with each child on an individual basis. Take a picture of the child holding or reading his or her book. It will make the student feel cared for by you and pleased to see that some of his or her positive attributes are being noticed and appreciated by someone in authority.

What Do You Think?

Ms. Schwartz teaches kindergarten in a small rural community. Her mother and father were both teachers, and she grew up loving to read. She is surprised that the children in her classroom do not seem very interested in books. At free time, they never pick up a book, and they often seem distracted when she is reading to them. What would you suggest to Ms. Schwartz?

a   Borrow numerous books from the library. Put them all around the room. Pick selections from several to read to children at different times throughout the day. Eventually they will hear one they like and will become more interested.

b   Make reading a really special time for children. Involve them in the selection of the books you read to them. Explore the book before you read it together. Look at the pictures and try to imagine what the book will be about. Talk about the story and who the characters remind you of. Model asking questions of the text, and encourage the children to do the same.

c   Give the students reading homework. Require parents to read with their children every night for 15 minutes, Keep a log of the stories the children have read together with their parents. At the end of each quarter, have a special celebration for the children and parents who read the most books.

The correct answer is (b). Many children come to school not knowing how enjoyable reading can be. They may also have little experience knowing how to read in a purposeful way. Research tells us although having access to books is important (a), it is the relationship that forms between the adult and child who are reading together that improves children's literacy skills (Bus & van Ijzendoom, 1995). Reading programs that are contingent on parent participation (c) can be very embarrassing and shameful to children living in families marred by family violence, as well as those whose parents cannot read. They have little control over getting their parents to read with them.

Addressing Language Concerns

As discussed in Chapter 3, children traumatized by violence often live in families whose communication style is not conducive to language growth. The stress within the family and the tendency toward limited conversational speech result in receptive and expressive language issues that need to be addressed as part of literacy instruction. Like other at-risk children with language problems, traumatized children benefit from classroom environments that are rich in opportunities for teacher-modeled conversation and frequent opportunities to talk with teachers and peers (Frey & Fisher, 2004). These activities help children improve their spoken language skills, specifically the abilities to speak about themselves and to tell a story using a sequential structure. They provide an excellent scaffold for reading instruction by building vocabulary and teaching children to use language purposefully.

Tyrone is one of several children in my classroom who has gaps in oral language abilities. The school's reading specialist suggested that I use book clubs as part of my literacy instruction to help these children practice their communication skills and become more comfortable using academic language (Raphael & McMahon, 1994). Each club is a small heterogeneous group of children that meets with me twice a week to discuss the book we are reading together. We have a great time. I bring a snack to share during our discussion, and everyone is pretty relaxed.

Prior to the meeting, children read the portion of the text we are going to discuss and they record their ideas in a reading log. We use the logs to get the conversation going. We talk about things we thought about while reading the text and share our ideas about its meaning to us. It is such an enjoyable way to practice language skills and at the same improve reading and comprehension skills. Tyrone loves attending, and every week he contributes a little more. He's become much more confident and much more fluent in his use of academic language.

Managing Behavior

The effects of trauma on children's capacity for self-regulation and emotional control can interfere with literacy acquisition by reducing the amount of instructional time available to them or by limiting their ability to attend to instruction or complete tasks in a timely manner. The externalizing behaviors sometimes exhibited by these children are disruptive to classroom order. When these students are removed from the classroom until behaviors are brought under control, they lose valuable instructional time (Arnold, 1997; Shores & Wehby, 1999). Obviously, this affects acquisition of important literacy skills and limits opportunities to participate in literature circles or story sharing activities that help them understand story structure and language.

It is important to have trauma-sensitive approaches to behavior management in place so children do not miss literacy instruction because of their behavior. Care must be given to establishing a learning environment that provides children with the emotional support they need to be successful. Traumatized children need to feel cared for and supported by their classroom teachers. Without this type of nurturing relationship, the demands of learning how to read may exceed the children's capacity to cope.

Anxiety and intrusive thoughts can also interfere with children's ability to participate in literacy instruction. Extended periods of quiet time or individual paper and pencil tasks are very difficult for children who struggle to control feelings of fear and helplessness. They may find it difficult to concentrate in the absence of a more interactive instructional format. These children benefit from literacy activities that involve movement, music, storytelling, and opportunities for peer interaction. The creativity and sense of emotional well-being that flow from these types of experiences help children stay connected to the lesson rather than being overcome by stress and worry.

What You Can Do

- Institute "Fancy Fridays." These are days when the teacher and a select group of children, instead of having a cafeteria lunch, have a special lunch in an area of the room that is set up like a restaurant with a tablecloth, napkins, and silverware. Teachers, and sometimes speech-language pathologists, model appropriate social conversation. Children attend Fancy Fridays on a rotating basis so no one is excluded.

- Have group storytelling time, during which one person gets the story going and then hands a baton or scarf to another child. That person adds a sentence that is on topic. The story continues until the group has told a story with at least five to ten sentences that are on topic and that moves through the sequence of beginning, middle, and end. As the children are creating their story, the teacher records it. At the end, she asks questions from the text that allow further elaboration of the themes.

- Use Mad Libs with children. These story frames with missing words can be pur-chased in any children's bookstore. Once a Mad Lib story is selected, the teacher starts reading it, pauses whenever a word needs to be supplied, and gives each child a turn to provide a word. As the Mad Lib is filled in, no one except the teacher knows what the story is about. He or she simply asks for a part of speech, and the child replies with whatever word comes to mind. At the end, the teacher reads the story, often with hysterical results. Mad Libs are a great way for chil-dren to explore language in a playful, nonthreatening way.
- Provide opportunities for children to have reading partners.
- Use classroom projects that require children to read directions for completion.
- Have children practice reading by learning the words to folk songs, Broadway show tunes, or other music that they enjoy. Have them do research on the history of the music they select and tell the class what they learned.
- Have word games such as Scrabble available as anchoring activities that children can do when they have free time.

What Do You Think?

Mr. Andrews is concerned about Julie, a girl in his second-grade classroom who never seems to finish any of her reading or spelling assignments. She is not overly disrup-tive, but she spends a lot of time sharpening her pencil or leaving to see the school nurse. As a result, Mr. Andrews has very few reading grades for Julie. What would you suggest that he do?

a   Meet with Julie and explain the situation. Tell her that you are willing to accept her work late but that she has to complete at least four of the eight assignments. She can pick the ones she will do.

b   Call Julie's mother and arrange for her to pick up Julie an hour later every Tuesday, Wednesday, and Thursday for the next 2 weeks. Stay after school with Julie to help her finish her reading assignments. She may just need the extra attention.

c   Rethink the assignments you are giving Julie to develop her reading skills. Give her an interest inventory to find out what kind of things she would like to read about. Then ask Julie what kinds of activities she would like to use to show you what she's learned. Schedule times when the two of you can discuss her work and see how it is progressing.

The correct answer is (c). Although both (a) and (b) both offer a solutions to Julie's short-term problem, neither one is going to make her an interested and involved reader. For that to happen, Mr. Andrews needs to gain access to Julie's interests so he can develop materials that are meaningful to her.

MEDIATED LEARNING
EXPERIENCES IN LITERACY INSTRUCTION

What You Know	You know that mediated learning experiences with caring adults help children learn to be purposeful readers.
What's New	Traumatized children often lack a history of mediated learning experiences, making it more difficult for them to become purposeful readers.

Interactions between parents and children marred by family violence are often so inconsistent that children have no one to guide their thinking and behavior. Their parents are not able to interpret the meaning of the children's experiences or help with strategies to manage problems. In fact, many of these children function as their own parent and struggle by themselves to acquire the vocabulary and cognitive strategies needed to explore and respond to the world around them. As a result, they lack any systematic method for acquiring new information. Like other at-risk populations of learners, these children benefit significantly from instruction that taps into the cognitive processes that underlie reading (Tovani, 2000). This type of instruction helps fill the gaps that occur in children's conceptual understanding of the world when their early experience is not mediated by the presence of a caring adult. Support in organizing information in a systemic manner and acquiring cognitive strategies enables them to take more control of their learning.

These children benefit from relationships with adults who help them learn reading concepts and skills. When teachers and other staff members are prepared to play a mediating role in the learning process, they can help children acquire the missing links in their cognitive development brought on by the lack of early collaborative experiences (Feuerstein, 1980). Teachers and children work together, exploring and understanding data gathered from a variety of sources: personal experience, literature, current events, and content subjects. The adult mediates the child's learning by sharing her own mental models and systems of exploration as a way of helping the child acquire his own. This is an effective way for teachers to engage children and help them improve their sense of competence and control in approaching academic tasks. Eventually these mediated learning experiences expand to include sharing text and content area information. Teachers help children interpret what they see and link it to other events or experiences in their lives. With support and practice, children build a framework for exploring their environment in a systematic, purposeful manner. This includes a conceptual understanding of how knowledge is acquired and strategies for anticipating and solving problems (Payne, 1996). These supportive interactions with teachers result in children assuming greater control over their own learning, an important first step in acquiring a sense of control in other areas of their lives as well.

I use core concepts as the basis for all my instruction. I tell the children we are learning to read using the scientific method! We look at what we are about to read; then, based on what we know about the author, how the page is set up, what the illustrations look like, and what the title and table of contents say, we create a hypothesis for reading. In the beginning, we all "test" the same hypothesis, but as children get more confident, we sometimes generate two or three different hypotheses and then determine which one is most strongly supported in the text. It is so much fun!

After we decide on the hypothesis, we start our data collection. I tell the children, it's like the television show CSI. *You have to search carefully for clues. I tell them to be sure to look for hidden clues and unexpected relationships. They take notes on their data, usually working in pairs or in small groups. Sometimes children need to move beyond the actual text, using the Internet or content-area textbooks as backup for inferences they think they can draw from the text.*

Then we are ready for our lab. We collate each small group's findings, using Venn diagrams to compare and contrast their work. After reviewing all of the findings, we check back on our original hypothesis. If we made an accurate prediction, we celebrate with a special snack and hang a "success certificate" on our "The Science of Reading Wall." If our hypothesis was wrong, we talk about what misled us and how to avoid making that kind of error in the future. It's a great strategy for helping children integrate many of the concepts and skills they need for reading while working together and enjoying one another's company.

Comprehending Text

Comprehending text involves the ability to simultaneously extract and construct meaning through interaction and involvement with written language (RAND Reading Study Group, 2002). It is a process whereby reader and author collaborate to arrive at a deeper meaning. Once children learn how this collaboration works, they search for clues that the author has integrated into the text, combining textual information with their own background knowledge to construct their own meaning.

Children traumatized by family violence may have limited background experiences to draw on when undertaking a comprehension task. They need teachers to provide more information to them about the subject they are reading about. They also need more direction in recognizing what they already know about a topic. Many children have difficulty making connections to prior knowledge because they think they are being asked about personal experiences. These children benefit from drawing a distinction between knowledge and experience, in addition to thinking through the many ways they might know about something that they have never experienced (Tovani, 2000).

What You Can Do

- Provide explicit instruction in perceiving patterns and connections in text. Help children notice the structure of the literary genre that they are reading. Have them categorize pages of text by structure rather than topic area.
- Schedule times to ask students if they would like additional help with a certain skill. This lets children know that you are interested in them and are available to support them rather than judge them.
- Provide children with reading materials that contain more complex narratives and language structures than those found in remedial texts. Even children who are at

the decoding level of reading can benefit from being part of a literature circle, listening to and interacting with a well-written story.

- Provide children with access to age-appropriate magazines that give them opportunities to read and appreciate nonfiction.

Shared Reading

Shared reading experiences are particularly helpful to traumatized children when the activities include the mediating presence of the teacher—helping the children uncover the pattern of relationships underlying a story line or calling attention to details they might have overlooked. This type of mediated learning develops a systematic framework for approaching text while giving children opportunities to improve their comprehension and fluency skills.

As children become more proficient in interpreting text, other types of shared reading experiences, such as reciprocal or dialogic reading, deepen children's understanding of these concepts. These experiences sharpen their ability to use the social context of a group to arrive at shared interpretations of meaning (Marzano, Pickering, & Pollack, 2001).

Tyrone is much more purposeful in his reading if he is involved in a reciprocal reading group (Palinscar & Brown, 1984). He is one of four children in the group. Each child plays a different role in relation to the text the group is reading. One summarizes what the group has just read, highlighting "big ideas" that others can add to as the discussion continues. Another child shares the questions that occurred to him or her while reading. Some of this student's questions can be answered directly from the text, but others rely on the prior knowledge of the other group members. Sometimes a question needs to be researched further by using the Internet or other additional sources. A third child is responsible for helping the group clarify confusing parts of what they've just read, while the fourth child asks the group to predict what might happen next. The predictions are written on our reading chart; when we complete the next section, we refer to these recorded predictions to see if they were correct.

Tyrone has gotten really good at generating questions, and I've noticed that he will sometimes get a book from the library that gives more information about what he wants to know. I think listening to the other children make predictions has improved his ability to plan ahead. Participating in the group helps him focus and take control of what he is accomplishing here at school.

What Do You Think?

Ms. Marsico wants to help her students improve their reading and writing skills. Until now, most of their reading instruction has focused on decoding. Ms. Marsico wants them to learn how to take pleasure in what they read. Where do you think she should start?

a   A lot of the classic children's stories are now available in a simplified reading format. The sentence structure is less complex, and the stories are not told in the same detail as the original version. The children could probably read them independently and feel good about their progress.

b   Do a reading inventory to determine the children's reading levels. Then, provide each child with a lot of books for his or her independent reading level.

c   Have the children select something that they would like to read that is slightly above their independent reading level. Arrange time to read each of the children's books with them, providing scaffolds as necessary, to arrive at a shared meaning of the text.

The correct answer is (c). Children become better readers when adults continue to mediate their reading instruction, helping them work in their zone of proximal development: the area between their independent reading level and their level of potential development (Vygotsky, 1986). Although using simplified texts (a) may be useful in some situations, this approach runs the risk of reinforcing some traumatized children's negative beliefs about their inability to do anything well. Reading only at their independent level (b) does not help them improve their skills.

STRATEGY INSTRUCTION

What You Know	You know that children who have strategies for approaching text are capable of comprehending text in an accurate and efficient manner.
What's New	When children grow up in unpredictable environments, they often need direct instruction in strategic reading to help them approach text in a purposeful manner.

Children trying to manage the traumatizing consequences of family violence are often unfocused or distracted readers. Chronic feelings of helplessness, coupled with anxiety and worry about their safety, cause them to give up easily. This is especially true when they must trust their ability to reach a logical conclusion based on clues in the text or with the personal connections made with the story. It is beneficial when these students can work with a teacher to develop strategies for constructing meaning from text, because such strategies give children the tools they need to take control of their own reading. The success derived from using strategies is well documented (Pressley, 2000). Strategies help children grow more confident in their ability to achieve mastery through personal effort (Alvermann, 2005). This enhances their perceptions of self-efficacy and encourages them to keep working toward academic competence. Although there are many strategies for reading instruction, the strategy of connecting with text has particular relevance to children trying to manage the traumatizing consequences of violence. Other important literacy activities include learning how to ask questions of the text and setting goals.

Connecting with Text

Children traumatized by family violence often lack the self-awareness needed to make connections between what they are reading and their own experience. Or, the literature that is available to them is so divorced from their day-to-day lives that they cannot relate to the characters or story line. This seriously compromises their reading ability, because learning how to comprehend depends on making connections with text—the process through which children derive meaning from stories by applying their own ideas to them (Wooten & Cullinan, 2004). Making connections helps children visualize the action, interact with the author, and bring their own meaning to the words.

Helping traumatized children acquire this important reading strategy requires literacy instruction that is grounded in quality children's literature. It incorporates activities that allow children to build off one another's ideas and provides frequent opportunities for reflection and feedback.

Quality children's literature uses traditional stories from around the world to address difficult issues. These stories help children grapple with the painful aspects of life by exploring how people throughout the ages have faced adversity and moved through it (Fredericks, 1997). With the support of each other's ideas, children recall forgotten past experiences and begin to connect the text they are currently reading with books or activities they have encountered before. Opportunities for reflection and feedback help them become more aware of their own thinking process and more confident of their ability to understand and interpret text.

Tyrone never seems to be able to make a connection to what we are reading in class. Whenever I ask him about what he knows about a topic, he says, "I don't know." If I push him at all, he just shuts down and I have trouble reengaging him. The reading specialist suggested that I try a more cooperative activating activity to see if the other children's ideas help Tyrone come up with a few of his own.

I started putting the theme of the day's shared reading on the board every morning. As I did the morning busywork—collecting lunch tickets, taking attendance, and so forth—I asked the children to go the board and write down anything they could think of that related to the topic. It was kind of like a "visual brainstorming" session. Tyrone didn't contribute anything at first, but after a few days I noticed that he had contributed two ideas. We were on our way. I think it is just a safer way for him to participate. He doesn't have to talk. He doesn't even have to acknowledge that the ideas are his, but I think he feels proud that he has something to contribute.

What You Can Do

- Stock your classroom library with a diversity of books so children can choose from a range of genres and topics.
- Model how you connect with what you have read. Make a transparency of a passage from a book that you are reading. As you read the passage, write down the connections you make. Share these with the children (Tovani, 2000).
- Provide students with frequent opportunities for interactive notetaking. For each major topic in their notes, have the students draw a symbol that stands for what they have written. Creating the symbols reinforces the concepts children are learning and allows the information to be stored in both the linguistic and motor areas of the brain.
- Use reader's theatre to make an emotional connection with a text. Have the students select a passage to act out, using props and costumes that they believe reflect the meaning of the text.

What Do You Think?

Ms. Bellafiore teaches third grade in a school where children come from diverse cultural backgrounds. She wants the students to make meaningful connections with text but is not sure where to start. What would you suggest to her?

a   Flood your classroom with different versions of the same children's story, told through the eyes of different cultures. Have the children compare and contrast the ways different authors tell the same story.

b   Instead of having children do independent seat work, have them work with a partner to read the text together and support one another's efforts to making meaningful connections to the text. Have them complete a culminating activity together that summarizes what they have learned.

c   Both (a) and (b).

The correct answer is (c). Reading versions of familiar stories that reflect children's cultural heritage and encouraging them to work together on reading tasks gives children the emotional support they need to feel safe and respected.

Asking Questions of the Text

The random, episodic manner in which traumatized children tend to remember information often translates to an unfocused approach to reading, slowing them down and making answers to specific comprehension questions difficult. Unfocused readers are likely to miss details or reach conclusions that are not substantiated in the text. When this happens, they become frustrated and more entrenched in their conviction that they are incapable and helpless.

To help children stay more focused during reading, work with them to develop a list of questions about the text before they start to read. When students are required to find the answers to their questions and to document them, they read in a more motivated and purposeful way. The questions are mediated by the teacher, who models the strategy that he or she wants the children to use: asking his or her own questions or generating questions from the children by pointing out words in the title or first sentence. Book covers and illustrations also are sources of questions about the text, as is a review of other books by the same author.

Asking questions of the text as they read means that children more fully grapple with the meaning of what they are reading. Questioning helps them distinguish between answers that are clearly stated in the text and those that are only implied. This helps students deduce the answer based on the author's clues and their own prior knowledge (Raphael & McMahon, 1994; Tovani, 2000).

What You Can Do

- Provide children with question-making stems that are a part of a question they might ask to make meaning from text. For example, "When _____ happened, why did _____?" (Payne, 1996, p. 137).
- Brainstorm your questions about a topic in front of the class, recording things you wonder about (Tovani, 2000).
- Work with students to create poetry out of authentic questions (Heard, as cited in Tovani, 2000).
- Model asking questions about something that you are reading.
- Provide guided practice in asking questions.

Setting Goals

Traumatized children are described as those who act instead of plan (van der Kolk, 2001). Repeated experiences of having no control over what happens to them leaves children incapable of knowing how to plan a course of action to achieve a specific goal. The behavior of many of these children suggests that they do not care about school or about learning how to read. The reality is that although they care, they can see no way to improve their performance or change the circumstances in their lives (Cole et al., 2005).

Teaching these children to set goals helps them overcome their helpless attitude and acquire a conceptual understanding of the relationship between effort and achievement. This requires that teachers instruct them in task analysis and action planning. Children need opportunities to solve real-life problems or investigate meaningful personal interests as part of their literacy instruction. Consistent use of these strategies, coupled with specific feedback from teachers on the progress they are making, helps children approach reading with greater confidence and improve their overall comprehension ability (Schunk & Rice, 1993).

What You Can Do

- Create a rubric for effort. Review the rubric's essential elements with the children. Talk to them about criteria for performance indicating insufficient, adequate, and exceptional levels of effort. Post the rubric where children can refer to it on an as-needed basis.
- Provide a rubric that specifies the characteristics of the quality of work expected.
- Periodically provide children with opportunities to evaluate their effort in performing various academic tasks. Have them graph the relationship between different levels of effort and changes in their achievement.
- Give children certificates for effort.
- Provide direct instruction on how to analyze the reading tasks that students are expected to complete. Scaffold additional supports as appropriate to ensure their success. Have the children estimate the time they think it will take to complete each segment of the task.

- Assign children a goal in reading a passage of text. Ask them to make note of the parts of the text they used to achieve the assigned goal. Provide specific feedback about the progress they are making.

- Tell stories about people setting goals and the effort it took to achieve them. Encourage children to tell similar stories from their own family or personal experiences.

What Do You Think?

Mr. McManus teaches fifth grade, a school year when children start receiving long-term assignments. He knows that many of his students have problems at home, so he made arrangements with the after-school program leader to let his students work on the projects as one of their after-school activities. Mr. McManus also gives them time to work on their projects on Thursday and Friday afternoons, but he still has children who cannot finish anything on time. What suggestions would you make to Mr. McManus?

a   Make sure the students have a rubric that gives them a clear date when each part of the project is due. If they do not make the deadline, let them work on the project during recess.

b   Before you start your next project, give children an opportunity to learn more about the passage of time and how to estimate it more precisely. Let them pick a task each day. Ask them to estimate the length of time they think it will take to complete each step and to write down the estimate. Then, set a timer. Turn it off when each step is done. Have the children compare their estimates with the actual length of time for each step.

c   It sounds like you have been very supportive to the students. Maybe they are taking advantage of you. Tell them that from now on, they will lose full credit for any section of the project that is not handed in on time.

The correct answer is (b). Many children who live in families where there are no consistent routines have trouble understanding the passage of time. They need practice in understanding the concept of time and in estimating the length of time needed to complete a task before they can successfully complete long-term projects on time. Although giving children time within the school day to complete work may solve the short-term problem (a), it will do nothing to help them acquire the underlying skill. Likewise, withdrawing your support and punishing them for their inability to meet a deadline (c) will do nothing to improve their conceptual understanding of time and may negatively affect their motivation to succeed.

WRITING INSTRUCTION

What You Know	You know that putting words to paper can be difficult for many children. They may be afraid that they do not know the "right" answer or that their work will reflect what they do not know.
What's New	Traumatized children may be afraid that what they write will reveal something about themselves or their family that will get them in trouble. They may be too unaware of their own thoughts and feelings to complete writing assignments that require a personal response.

Writing can be an extremely stressful part of literacy instruction for children who are traumatized by family violence. Because these children are consumed with keeping the secrets of family violence, they have little remaining energy to measure up to school expectations for writing and self-expression (Horsman, 2000). These children are struggling, not only with the trauma of family violence, but also with their need to hide it. They fear that their stories will reveal something that other people are not supposed to know. This leads to "stopping and starting" writing behaviors that look like a lack of motivation, threaten task completion, and make teachers think children are not trying. In fact, these behaviors may actually reflect a child's efforts to find a middle ground between his or her actual experiences at home and the writing assignment. It is difficult to write authentically on the theme "What I Did on the Weekend" when in fact what the child did over the weekend was get hit in the face with a belt or watch one parent push the other down the stairs.

Children traumatized by family violence lack the self-awareness they need to write well. Their attention is so focused on the behavior of others that assignments requiring them to discuss their own feelings or personal reactions to stories they have read paralyze them—they are afraid that their answers are wrong or that they may be misunderstood. Initially these children benefit from writing about classroom experiences as they happen. One example might be working with a peer to record observations of which playground equipment was used most frequently during recess. Observing which foods people chose most often at lunch or snack allows the writing process to begin while avoiding its potentially emotional consequences. These simple, classroom-based writing assignments are a safe, manageable way to teach children how to use language to mediate experiences.

I knew that writing would be hard for Tyrone, because the topic starters at this grade level have a lot to do with home and family. I was afraid these would be too emotionally charged for him, so I started giving children ways to write about those topics in a more impersonal way. For example, they could write about their own family trip or the family trip we read about. Tyrone always picked the more impersonal topic, but that was okay. He really improved in his ability to get things down on paper. He's now able to write five or six sentences on topic, and sometimes he even shares what he's written with the class. I think he's really proud of the progress he's made.

As children grow confident in the safety of the classroom and in their ability to write precisely and accurately, they benefit from using journals in content areas such as math and science. Journaling in these subjects gives students a safe way to record the process they used to arrive at their answers. It helps them gain insight into how they think and gives them practice in using words to describe their experiences in a safe, protected manner that does not probe into feelings or internal states. Eventually children are introduced to the practice of using journals to record personal feelings and observations. Safety is maintained by offering a range of topics to journal about, as well as a choice of an audience to read the journals.

The importance of helping traumatized children acquire writing skills cannot be emphasized enough. In the right environment, writing is a powerful tool for regaining the sense of control, connection, and meaning that has been lost through trauma (Horsman, 2000). It helps children describe their experiences as distinct from themselves, which in turn enables students to begin making new meaning of the adversity in their lives and helps them arrive at new levels of self-control and hope.

What You Can Do

- Use storyboards to help children sequence their writing.
- Write stories in small groups, with each child contributing several sentences on the same topic. Have children work together to ensure that the ideas are correctly sequenced and that story has a clear beginning, middle, and end.
- Introduce children to journal writing. Give them the choice of having their journals be "for their eyes only" or a means of communicating back and forth with you or another child. Sometimes children like to share some journal entries but prefer to keep others private. In that case, give them the option of putting an "OK" on the pages they want you to read.
- Set up a pen pal program and give children the option to participate. Pen pals can use traditional letter writing or e-mail communication to share their thoughts and feelings and establish a relationship. A pen pal program can target certain audiences. For example, younger children can write to older children, or children can write to residents of a local assisted living facility.

What Do You Think?

Ms. Sampson loves using the writing workshop model with her children (Calkins, 2001). She finds that it is a great way to engage children in expressing their thoughts and feelings in a comfortable, nonthreatening manner. She has noticed, however, that one girl, Marcy, refuses to participate. Ms. Sampson is puzzled because Marcy is a good reader and has no trouble with penmanship. What would you tell Ms. Sampson?

a   This is probably just a phase Marcy is going through. Encourage her to use pictures to create stories until she is comfortable using words.

b   Marcy may feel she is not getting enough attention. Offer her some special time with you as an incentive for her to write more.

c   It is possible that Marcy is afraid of revealing some family secrets in her writing. Provide her with a choice of topics that include writing about school-related experiences.

The correct answer is (c). In a trauma-sensitive classroom environment, children should always be offered a choice of writing topics. Topic choices should include the option to write about school-related experiences. Although the need for more attention (a) or a preference for other expressive modalities (b) may also influence children's writing, it is important to keep in mind that for some children the need to keep family secrets may be affecting their writing production.

CONCLUSION

A trauma-sensitive approach to reading and writing instruction provides children with opportunities to experience the pleasure of shared reading in the company of a caring adult. Teachers use mediated learning experiences to produce purposeful readers and precise, accurate writers. Care is given to provide children with the emotional safety and support they need so that they can focus on what they are doing and be successful. Comprehension strategies are introduced and practiced within a social context; in turn, that encourages collaboration with one another to arrive at a better understanding of what they are reading. Children are then better able to use what they are learning to set and achieve personal goals.

7

Managing the Emotional Demands of Teaching

The ability of children to deal with trauma depends to a large extent on the coping skills of the adults around them. Supportive adults who are able to respond to problems in a calm and thoughtful manner are an important resource for children struggling to cope with the adversity in their lives. This chapter addresses how teachers can help children make a healthy adaptation to their stress by ensuring that their own physical, psychological, and spiritual health is not neglected.

Beth Anne was the first child I taught whom I knew had been abused. She had been removed from her home and was living with her aunt and uncle. She was so young and had been through so much already. I decided the best thing I could do for her was to help her enjoy first grade and teach her how to read. It was tough, but I hung in there with her.

I recently met her aunt in the grocery store. She told me that Beth Anne still talks about the fun she had in my classroom. She told her aunt that what she remembers best is how safe she felt with me. She never had to worry about bad things happening—so she could just relax and be herself. Beth Anne knew I'd take care of her. Stories like that keep you going as a teacher; they let you know you are making a difference in children's lives.

ENGAGING CHILDREN IN POSITIVE WAYS

What You Know	You know that being emotionally connected to the children you are teaching facilitates their learning and social development.
What's New	Teaching traumatized children involves a willingness to help them contain patterns of traumatic reenactment that limit their ability to move beyond past experiences.

Reparative experiences with teachers help children recover from the effects of violence and trauma (Solomon, 2003). Teachers restore children's sense of hope and purposefulness. They help children move beyond the adversity experienced in their homes. And, just as important, teachers are instrumental in helping children acquire social and academic competencies. These are necessary to contain the developmental psychopathology that can result from childhood stress and trauma (Masten & Coatsworth, 1995).

Beth Anne had no experience working with an adult to change behaviors or correct misunderstandings. She seemed so anxious, trying to please me even when she was angry or upset. She was so afraid of being rejected by me. It took her a long time to realize that I was on her side, that I was there to help her rather than criticize or shame her.

Giving Children a Second Chance

Positive relationships with teachers give children a second chance—a second chance to experience the coregulation necessary to develop self-regulation. Collaboration with adults helps children gain control over their feelings. It gives them the attention they need to develop the foundation for personal agency—an important aspect for success in school.

However, this work requires a level of emotional detachment that is sometimes difficult for teachers to maintain. Although most teachers understand that their role can trigger unresolved parental issues for some children, they may be unprepared for the intense interactions that can be unleashed between themselves and children traumatized by family violence. Exposure to violence or relational trauma causes children to repeatedly reenact past traumatic experiences with teachers and other caring adults (Farragher & Yanosy, 2005). Without proper training, teachers can unintentionally perpetuate the patterns of destructive repetition that characterize the original trauma (Bentovim, 1992). To avoid getting caught in an endless loop of destructive repetition, teachers need skills to manage the double struggle of controlling their own emotions and behavior and de-escalating the children's emotions and behavior. Otherwise they run the risk of *mirroring* the children's behavior rather than *modeling* emotional regulation and control (Long, 1998).

As a teacher, I take pride in my ability to stay objective and not get hooked into power struggles with children. I work really hard at redirecting the children's behavior and usually don't take things personally. But with Beth Anne it was different. I sometimes felt like she was setting me up to behave in ways that reinforced her belief that all adults are unfair or hostile.

My interactions with her were beginning to make me feel incompetent until the school psychologist helped me understand what was happening. She explained that children who are abused often try to engage adults in a power struggle as a way of protecting themselves from the rejection they fear will occur when their "essential badness" is exposed. They do not believe that a positive relationship with an adult is possible.

The psychologist encouraged me to stay calm with Beth Anne and not rush in to prove how much I cared for her. She reminded me that my job was not to rescue Beth Anne but to help her develop her own adaptive capacities to manage the stress in her life. That conversation really helped me avoid getting caught in Beth Anne's feelings of helplessness and despair. I came to see my role as one of offering her the possibility of things getting better, of relationships being safe.

What Do You Think?

Ms. Kydon teaches kindergarten in a school that enrolls many children who have histories of abuse and neglect. She is very sensitive to the difficulties in their lives and works hard to help them succeed. Most children are doing quite well, but a few continue to have tantrums. This is discouraging to Ms. Kydon. She sometimes wonders if she is capable of working with children whose behavior is so difficult to control. What would you tell her?

a   The children who are still having tantrums are probably not ready for school. They need to get their behavior under control before you can be expected to instruct them.

b   Teaching children who are out of control is emotionally draining. Do not try to do it alone. Plan for back-up support when a tantrum happens, as well as time to process your feelings with the principal or school psychologist.

c   Request that a one-to-one paraprofessional be assigned to any child who continues to have tantrums. That way when a tantrum occurs, the paraprofessional can remove the child from the classroom until the behavior is brought under control.

The correct answer is (b). Teachers need support to help them manage their reactions to children whose behavior is emotionally draining. This should include help managing the behavior as well as time to process how it is affecting them. Children should not be segregated in school because of the trauma they have suffered at home (a). Classrooms are an appropriate context for children to acquire self-regulation, but it does not happen quickly. Teachers need to know that additional support is available as needed so that instruction is not disrupted. Although paraprofessionals are an important source of support in public schools, care should be taken not to give them the primary responsibility of managing children's behavior (c). This can limit the paraprofessional's role in the classroom and may inadvertently reinforce children's feelings of helplessness.

CHANGING PERCEPTIONS

What You Know	You know that trauma causes changes in children's cognitive understanding of themselves, others, and their environment.
What's New	Working with traumatized children can change a teacher's perception of him- or herself and the children in the classroom.

Teachers are often the first, and sometimes the only, adults to witness when children are stressed or in danger. They offer children feedback about the difficulty of their situation while integrating stories of hope and survival into classroom activities and routines. They are in a unique position to talk to children about how people manage adversity in a resilient manner. They can tell stories about fictional characters who live in violent situations and offer strategies for buffering the effects of this experience on peer relationships and skill development.

An effective witness must acknowledge the difficulty of the child's position without getting caught up in the accompanying feelings of hopelessness and compromised sense of meaning. Teachers need training in empathizing with the child and his or her situation rather than actually experiencing what the child is feeling. Responding in this manner allows the teacher to stay emotionally connected to the child while maintaining sufficient objectivity. This then allows the introduction of alternative ways of thinking or behaving that might make the child feel better. This type of "situational empathy" has the additional benefit of protecting the teacher's own internal state as he or she attends to the emotional needs of the child (Johnson, 2007).

I used to feel so bad when Beth Anne had a temper tantrum or melt-down. She seemed to have so many problems and not a lot of resources to fall back on. I'd find myself thinking about her all the time, sometimes waking up at night wondering if she was okay.

Then one day I realized that it wasn't doing her any good to have me as upset as she was. I asked the school psychologist for some advice, and she gave me an article about situational empathy. The article pointed out that we can have compassion for children without actually experiencing their feelings. In fact, by keeping some professional distance, we can actually help children more: We can be someone who shows them that life doesn't need to be so hard.

I decided I needed to establish some professional distance with Beth Anne. I stopped treating her like she had no control and instead, started showing her how to take control of some things at school. I helped her notice when she was feeling happy so she could remember what it felt like. We started a chart to record the times in the day that she felt happy or in control. This little technique helped her begin to see that she had some choices and that there was more in her life than the bad things that had happened to her at home. By taking control of my own emotions, I was able to help her take control of her own.

What You Can Do

- Use positive self-talk (e.g., "My feelings are a normal reaction to an abnormal situation").
- Avoid rash responses to questions or lightning-fast solutions to problems. Take time to form solutions. Breathe and think.
- Intervene only when children's behavior threatens their own safety or the safety of others or when one of the agreed-upon priority behaviors (previously decided by all members of the classroom) has been breached.
- Replace "you" statements (e.g., "You are . . .," "You need to get control of yourself") with "I" statements ("I feel . . . ," "I . . ."). This helps de-escalate conflict and provide reinterpretation of events that allow children to change and grow.
- When dealing with children in conflict, focus your energy on what the child needs from you at the moment rather than how you feel about him or her right now.

Teacher as Facilitator

Teachers are in a good position to observe children's interactions, noticing the children who are easily accepted by their peers, as well as those who may need help fitting in. Teachers help children gain greater acceptance by structuring classroom activities so children have opportunities to talk to one another, share perspectives, and come to appreciate one another. They create opportunities for students to practice social skills and become more confident in their ability to successfully negotiate social environments.

Although most teachers know how to encourage positive relationships among children, attending to the social needs of traumatized children sometimes proves a challenge. Many children are ignored or rejected by peers who view them as odd or aggressive (Pynoos, Steinburg, & Goenjian, 1996). Teachers may find it difficult to refrain from rescuing these students from uncomfortable social situations. They may need help providing children with the skills they need to establish themselves as valued members of their peer group.

What You Can Do

- Create opportunities for the children to achieve status in the classroom by assigning an important job or responsibility. These should be age appropriate, such as holding the flag for the Pledge of Allegiance or taking the ball to recess. Find opportunities to thank the children for their contribution to the class.

- Work with the school psychologist to integrate cooperative games and team-building activities into free time during lunch or recess. These games create interdependence between children and help those with underdeveloped social skills fit in more easily.

- Establish your classroom as a "bully-free zone." Have rules within the classroom that protect children's right to respect. Teach children to interact with one another in a caring, careful manner.

- Spend time each day discussing individual differences and exploring how they benefit your classroom and the larger society.

What Do You Think?

Ms. Switzer is quite concerned about the degree to which the children in her classroom are isolating one of the children in her fifth-grade homeroom. She notices that he is alone in homeroom and often skips lunch so he does not have to deal with being ignored in the cafeteria. What suggestions could you make to Ms. Switzer?

a   Talk to the child and tell him that you have noticed he always skips lunch in the cafeteria. Tell him he cannot be in the building unsupervised. Let him know that he can have lunch in the homeroom with you if he wants to.

b   Refer the child to the school psychologist. See if he can be placed in a social skills class or some other type of supportive environment to learn how to get along better with his peers.

c   Create a circle of friends that includes all children in the classroom. Anyone can request the additional support. Hold a circle meeting every morning to check in with children and see how they are watching out for one another.

The correct answer is (c). Ms. Switzer needs to work on building a classroom community where children learn how to accept and care for one another, even when they appear to have nothing in common. Although offering the child a chance to eat with her in the homeroom (a) is a kind thing to do, it does not help the child gain greater acceptance with his peers. Social skills training (b) might help this one student, but focusing only on his issues avoids the larger issue of community building and peer support.

EMOTIONAL DIMENSIONS OF TEACHING

What You Know	You know it is sometimes hard to make the transition from work to home. You spend a lot of time thinking about children's stories and worrying about their safety.
What's New	Teachers working with children exposed to violence often show signs of vicarious trauma, including nightmares, intrusive thoughts, and depression.

Teachers traditionally care for the social and emotional well-being of children, partnering with parents in developing the necessary social skills as well as academic competencies. This involvement with the emotional lives of families takes an emotional toll on teachers—often spilling over into their own personal lives. Unlike mental health agencies that take great care to protect the emotional well-being of individual therapists, schools have largely ignored the emotional well-being of teachers (Westling, Herzog, Cooper-Duffy, Prohn, & Ray, 2006). As a result, teachers are at risk of developing symptoms of burnout (Belcastro & Gold, 1983; Jackson, Schwab, & Schuler, 1986) or compassion fatigue (Jackson, 2004). These conditions are similar in the emotional exhaustion and helplessness that accompany them. Burnout causes teachers to lose enthusiasm for their work and question their ability to make a positive contribution to children's lives. Compassion fatigue is also characterized by feelings of incompetence, as well as difficulty maintaining a level of emotional detachment needed to manage feelings toward children whose behavior is repeatedly out of control.

Both conditions increase the likelihood of teachers making negative attributions about children's behavior (Bibou, Stogiannidou, & Kiosseoglou, 1999). This leads to escalation of conflict-ridden interactions and increases the chances of teachers unwittingly getting caught up in children's traumatic reenactments of past experiences with their parents or caregivers (Lamude, Scudder, & Furno-Lamude, 1992). In the case of compassion fatigue, professionals also experience such symptoms commonly seen in traumatized children: hyperarousal, nightmares, anxiety, and depression (Figley, 1995, 2003).

When I first started working with Beth Anne, I couldn't figure out what was wrong with me. I just knew I wasn't myself. I was tired all of the time and often found myself resenting how emotionally drained I felt at the end of the school day. I began to question my ability as a teacher.

It was such a relief to read an article on compassion fatigue and realize that how I felt was a normal reaction to the stories I was hearing—not only about Beth Anne's situation, but also about the problems some of my other children were having. My desire to help and make things better was wearing me out and compromising my ability to do my job well.

It was helpful to realize that there were things I could do to take care of myself. Now I make it a point to take 20–30 minutes at the end of the day to talk to my colleagues and make a plan for the next day.

Next, I'm off to the gym and then home to play with my children. Creating a boundary between work and home has really helped me gain perspective and avoid getting overwhelmed.

Personal and Professional Self-Renewal

Working with children who are suffering the traumatizing effects of family violence requires teachers to care for themselves. Teachers must engage in activities that are physically, emotionally, and spiritually rejuvenating. They need to garner professional support provided by team collaboration, integrated service delivery, and trauma-specific training and supervision.

Physical Rejuvenation

Responding to the needs of traumatized children demands a level of emotional availability and personal connection that is not sustainable without careful attention to one's physical health and well-being. This is particularly true of people working with children whose behavior is often characterized by hyperarousal and emotional dysregulation.

Daily physical exercise, nutritious meals, times of rest and relaxation, and adequate sleep are essential to a teacher's effectiveness, difficult though it may be to fit them into already crowded schedules. These essential elements help teachers maintain a necessary balance in their lives. This balance protects their health and serves as a safeguard against burnout and compassion fatigue—conditions that seriously compromise a teacher's sense of self-efficacy and emotional control.

What You Can Do

- Exercise daily. Take a walk during lunch or spend a few minutes stretching between classes.
- Take scheduled breaks, even if only for 3 minutes.
- Use stress management relaxation techniques to calm yourself.

- Combine exercise with something else you enjoy doing. If you like to have time alone to think about your day, build walking or yard work into your time for self-reflection. If you like to socialize with friends, arrange to take an exercise class together or play a team sport.
- Find ways of pampering yourself that help you relax and release the stress of the day. Schedule a facial or massage, take a hot bath, or ask your partner for a backrub.

Social/Emotional Rejuvenation

Just as physical activity restores a teacher's energy and state of well-being, opportunities to socialize with friends and loved ones provide the encouragement and joy needed to nurture children. Meaningful personal relationships sustain teachers and satisfy needs for attention, companionship, and, sometimes, hands-on assistance in managing the competing demands on teachers' time (Quarantelli & Dynes, 1977). Such relationships help teachers avoid personalizing children's behavior and maintain the emotional detachment needed to remain objective and to manage the double struggle.

The companionship of other professionals who share their enthusiasm for teaching is another important social support for teachers. This can occur through membership in professional organizations, as well as via the Internet or attendance at educational conferences and workshops. Participation in these types of activities restores teachers' interest in their profession. It solidifies being a member of a group whose shared mission is improving the lives of children. This sense of common purpose fosters feelings of efficacy and hope—feelings that are often lost in the day-to-day stress of teaching.

What You Can Do

- Know your limits. Know how much of your time and yourself you can give. Set limits and communicate them to others.
- Make use of social support. Reach out to friends, family, and co-workers.
- Find a way of processing how you are feeling as a result of your work with children. Write in your journal, or "debrief" with a trusted friend or colleague who listens to you with understanding rather than judgment.

- Connect to a cause or community group that is personally meaningful to you.
- Build a sense of professional connection with colleagues by attending workshops, using support groups, and meeting with colleagues to share coping strategies.
- Develop casual social relationships with other staff members. Help organize and participate in social events, such as shared lunches or after-school volleyball games.
- Celebrate successes.

What Do You Think?

Ms. Boley teaches eighth grade in a school that enrolls children from the local homeless shelter. Several of these children are in her classroom. Although she enjoys working with them, she finds their stories hard to listen to. Lately she has found herself feeling depressed at the end of the day. Instead of going to the gym after work, she is going home and crawling into bed, sometimes with a pizza or a bowl of ice cream. What advice would you give Ms. Boley?

a   Find a new job. The stress of working with so many troubled children is clearly getting to you.

b   Make plans to reconnect with friends. Schedule time for dinner together or a long walk on the beach.

c   Don't worry about a few early nights with a pizza or ice cream. Everybody has bad days. You will get over it.

The correct answer is (b). Teachers working with traumatized children need to be proactive in taking care of their physical and emotional health. One way to do this is to have regular contact with friends whom you enjoy being with and who help you relax. Feelings of stress (a) do not necessarily mean that the person is in the wrong job; they just mean that he or she needs to take better care of him- or herself. Although most people overindulge occasionally, overeating, especially alone, can mean that a person needs more support (c). It should not be allowed to go unnoticed.

Spiritual Rejuvenation

Working with children who struggle to adapt to adverse circumstances in their home or community challenges a teacher's long-standing beliefs about the meaning of life. Hearing multiple stories of children being victimized or abused leaves teachers feeling helpless and out of control. Taking time for some type of spiritual practice helps teachers restore their belief that there is meaning in what they are doing (Erikson, 1963).

Spiritual practices such as prayer, meditation, or yoga help teachers acquire the self-awareness they need to be effective with children. These practices get them in touch with their strengths and help them release the stress and anxiety that come from being overextended. They help teachers realize the limitations of their role while allowing them to recommit to helping children help themselves. Regular spiritual practice puts teachers in touch with children's resilience and their own sense of hope.

I've found that working with Beth Anne and other children who struggle with serious adversity has its own rewards. It has taught me a lot—how to be grateful for all of the blessings in my own life, how to be more compassionate with other people, and how to ask for help when I need it.

It's not a job you should do alone, but with the right support and training, I think most teachers find a great deal of satisfaction working with these children. You get to see their strength and courage—and celebrate their successes.

The children I work with are a real inspiration to me. They remind me of why I became a teacher. I really believe the work I am doing is making the world a better place. And that makes me really happy.

What You Can Do

- Learn to meditate. Incorporate 10–20 minutes of meditation into your daily routine.
- Create a specific list of healing activities. Look at the list regularly and update it every few weeks. Regularly commit to doing the things on the list.
- Limit your exposure to violent material by not watching violent movies or reading detailed accounts of gruesome events in newspapers or novels.
- Make self-renewal a part of everyday life. Set time aside each day to reconnect with yourself. Spend time working on a personal goal or hobby that helps you move forward in realizing a dream or developing a talent.

- Use a cleansing ritual to create a boundary between work and home. Take a walk, listen to soothing music, or use stretching exercises to ease the transition. If your position allows it, consider limiting the number of work-related telephone calls or e-mails that you respond to at home.

COLLABORATING WITH OTHER PROFESSIONALS

What You Know	You know that sharing and problem solving with other teachers help reduce the stress of teaching.
What's New	Teachers working with children exposed to violence need the support of a team, as well as opportunities to collaborate with mental health professionals who are knowledgeable about trauma.

Despite the key contributions teachers make to better the lives of traumatized children, they are seldom recognized as important partners in reversing the legacy of violence. They are not included in networks of psychologists and social workers providing services to children and families. They lack access to supports traditionally provided in clinical environments. Segregation from other professionals who serve the same population devalues teachers' work with traumatized children. It increases the social isolation and stress they already feel. This lack of support threatens not only their job performance, but also their sense of personal efficacy and emotional control.

I have several friends who are clinical social workers. They often invite me to workshops or lectures sponsored by the agencies they work for. I am amazed at how often the sessions are about preventing burnout or compassion fatigue. Schools never sponsor training on those topics. As teachers, we are so involved in other people's lives, yet there's not much information about how to manage our reactions to the problems faced by our students.

Team Collaboration

The social isolation that characterizes teaching often exacerbates the stress that teachers feel as they struggle to manage the demands of their job (Westling et al., 2006). Scheduling constraints or even the physical layout of a school can limit opportunities for adult contact, making informal networking and peer support difficult to achieve. Recent efforts at restructuring schools acknowledge the strain of teacher isolation and call for service delivery models that provide teachers with more team support (Adelman & Taylor, 2000, 2003; Connell & Klem, 2000; Elmore, 1996; McLaughlin & Mitra, 2001). Although these changes are primarily recommended as a way to improve student outcomes, they offer a framework upon which to scaffold additional supports. Teachers can then use these to replenish themselves and, in turn, manage their own emotional reactions to the life experiences of the children they are teaching.

School-Based Teams

School reform initiatives frequently recommend the formation of school-based teams that are composed of teachers and principals as well as various related service providers (e.g., school psychologists, speech-language pathologists, occupational therapists, physical therapists, school nurses, counselors, social workers). Teams work within a transdisciplinary structure, promoting collaboration, cross training, and shared responsibility for children's progress (Giangreco, 1994). Members share roles and responsibilities, purposely crossing disciplinary boundaries at each step of the instructional process: assessment, planning, intervention, and progress monitoring. This ensures a consistent approach to meeting children's needs and addressing teachers' concerns.

Teams use consensual decision making to reach agreement on their joint purpose as well as on the desired outcomes and methods for achieving them. Although it is time consuming, team decision making reduces the risk of miscommunication or the unintentional sabotaging of one another's efforts (Figley, 2003). Regularly scheduled team meetings provide a forum for members to review children's progress, make necessary changes to interventions, and resolve interpersonal issues as they occur.

Teams are an important resource for all teachers, especially those working with traumatized children. They reduce teachers' social isolation and help buffer the emotional effects of dealing with troublesome behaviors and reoccurring conflicts. Team feedback is a source of positive reinforcement for teachers, especially when they are feeling discouraged about children's progress (Han & Weiss, 2005). The perspectives of other team members celebrate the progress being made in developing children's strengths. This helps to avoid endless discussions of the difficulties inherent in working with children traumatized by family violence. Team feedback restores teachers' sense of self-efficacy and achievement. It allows them to stay focused on agreed-upon interventions and encourages them to think more positively about their impact on children's learning. As a result, they are able to stay more emotionally attuned to children's needs (Liston, Whitcomb, & Borko, 2006).

The thing I love most about team meetings is how much you learn at them. Beth Anne's team included me, a school psychologist, a speech-language pathologist, and an occupational therapist. We met once a week for about 45 minutes. But the communication didn't stop there! We wrote notes to each other, sent e-mails, and sometimes even talked on the phone. It was such a creative experience.

We always started our formal meetings with a review of what was going well. Then we'd review our agreed-upon interventions, clarifying any misunderstandings and making any necessary accommodations or changes. I learned so much about child development and how different people's training could be integrated into classroom experiences that would help Beth Anne acquire the competencies she needed.

Teams are particularly effective in managing the effects of splitting, a common pattern of traumatic reenactment. Children try to play adults off one another, by labeling some "good" and others "bad" or by challenging their interpretations of rules. The intent of the behavior is to keep adults at a distance by casting them once again in the role of untrustworthy caregivers. This has serious consequences on teacher morale (Long, 1998). It causes teachers to second-guess themselves and to question the trustworthiness of their colleagues. Regularly scheduled opportunities for meeting allows team members to check out facts and restore cohesion, thereby avoiding a disruption of team efforts at instruction and intervention.

Although the benefits of team collaboration in schools are clear, scheduling constraints and staff workloads make finding time a daunting task. School districts develop various approaches to the problem: Some schedule team meetings during the school day, using substitute teachers or back-to-back "specials" (e.g., art, music, physical education) to provide coverage; other districts provide extended days several times a month for team meetings or build time for team processing into regularly occurring staff or grade-level meetings.

In situations where there is no administrative support for teaming, teachers often create informal opportunities to give one another feedback. Although this approach is not as effective as regularly scheduled formal team meetings, these self-initiated gatherings help teachers avoid overreacting to student behaviors and restore their own sense of optimism and hope.

What You Can Do

- Arrange to have lunch once a week with one or more of the related service providers who work in your building. Use the time to brainstorm about how to make your classroom a comfortable and safe place for all children.

- Link with another teacher in your building to discuss ideas about how to address your concerns or to extend the benefits of successful activities.

- Prior to the beginning of the school year, ask your building principal to schedule specials in such way that you and related service providers share at least one free period a week that can be used for planning.

- Use e-mail or other forms of written communication for information exchange and other administrative tasks that are important but do not require face-to-face contact with other team members. This will give you more time for teaming and reaching agreed-upon priorities for intervention.

What Do You Think?

Ms. O'Brien is concerned about something that a student told her about a colleague, Ms. Hathaway. The child said that Ms. Hathaway had met her mother in the grocery store and told her not to worry about following the behavior plan that the mother had agreed to try. This student said that her mother quoted Ms. Hathaway as saying, "Those things never work anyway. We just write them to humor the psychologist." What you advice would you give to Ms. O'Brien?

a   Bring the issue to the team meeting. Find out what actually happened before drawing conclusions about Ms. Hathaway's trustworthiness.

b   Confront Ms. Hathaway with the information shared by the child. Ask her to defend her unethical behavior.

c   Let it go. This child has a history of telling lies. She is probably just trying to stir things up between her mother and the school.

The correct answer is (a). This may be a classic example of the type of splitting behavior in which a child engages when he or she is testing the trustworthiness of the adults who are caring for her. This student may be trying to stir up a controversy between her mother and two teachers on her team, thereby causing them to question their effectiveness and distract from the issues they are trying to help her address. Confronting Ms. Hathaway directly (b) assumes that she actually did what is being accused of. It also creates another splitting behavior when two team members try to resolve an issue by themselves rather than bringing it to the team. If all of the team members ignore the situation (c), they are giving up their responsibility to try to help the child resolve her issues.

Integrated Service Delivery

Integrated service delivery is another recommended school reform that increases opportunities for teaming and collaboration throughout the day. This model is decentralized in that the services occur where the child spends his or her day, rather than in a clinical or segregated setting. Integrated therapy and co-teaching are two examples of integrated service delivery that frequently occur in schools. These models reduce teacher isolation while creating positive instructional outcomes for children (Craig, Haggart, & Hull, 1999).

Integrated Therapy

The integrated therapy model was introduced into schools in the early 1990s as a way of responding to the needs of children with multiple disabilities within an educational setting (York, Rainforth, & Giangreco, 1990). The model uses cross training and consultation to help teachers accommodate the diverse needs of students. Initially the model focused on integrating the services of speech-language pathologists and occupational therapists into the classroom. More recently, however, school psychologists and other mental health workers have adopted the model as a preferred way of providing mental health services to children (Ringeisen, Henderson, & Hoagwood, 2003; Roans & Hoagwood, 2000). The model is associated with more positive child outcomes (Clarke, Hawkins, Murphy, & Sheeber, 1993), as well as long-term sustainability of interventions (Botvin, Schinke, Epstein, Diaz, & Botvin, 1995; Greenburg, Kusche, Cook, & Quamma, 1995; Hawkins, Catalano, Kosterman, Abbott, & Hill, 1999).

Using this model with traumatized children reduces the isolation experienced by teachers and helps them maintain a focus on agreed-upon priorities. Teachers and therapists meet regularly to identify areas of concern and possible interventions. Therapists adjust what they do in the classroom to address the concerns raised by the teacher. These adjustments include providing additional emotional support to children or working with small groups to improve their problem-solving or conflict resolution skills. Working together in this manner gives teachers and therapists the chance to regularly share observations and feedback, as well as to engage in hands on tweaking of the learning environment to accommodate individual children's needs. Teachers use interventions modeled by the therapist to provide children with support throughout the day in an agreed-upon, consistent manner.

What's really good about the integrated therapy model is that it brings teaming right into the classroom. We don't just talk about problems at team meetings. We work together in the classroom to figure things out. For example, at last week's team meeting, I talked about the fact that my children need visuals to remind them to use their words to express how they are feeling. So when the speech-language pathologist came to my class, she brought these great cue cards and posters she'd made. She showed the children how to use them, and we were on our way. The same thing happened last week when the school psychologist was in my room. She read a story, modeling techniques for eliciting perspective taking. Because I was in the room watching what the therapists were doing, I was able to integrate their strategies into my own lessons.

Co-teaching

Co-teaching is another model of integrated service delivery with the potential of reducing teachers' social isolation. It is similar to the integrated therapy model in the emphasis placed on collaboration and planning, as well as the presence of two professionals in the classroom working together with students.

Co-teaching infuses general education classrooms with the accommodations and supports needed to allow children with disabilities to successfully participate (Friend, 1996). Like integrated therapy, it is a capacity-building model in that the presence of the second adult, usually trained in special education, allows for accommodations to be made on an as-needed basis rather than after a history of demonstrated failure. This is a particularly beneficial aspect of the model for addressing the needs of traumatized children. Although many of these children demonstrate difficulties with academic or social competencies, they may not qualify for special education services. Their more subtle kinds of difficulty are easier to observe and respond to when there is a second teacher in the room.

Co-teaching, by definition, requires both adults to be equally responsible for the instruction of *all* children (Friend, 1996). Both adults plan for all children, as well as work with them directly. This co-teaching partnership offers several benefits to teachers working with traumatized children. It is an excellent way to build teachers' capacity to address the learning needs of these children while providing the social support necessary to avoid compassion fatigue or secondary trauma. Co-teaching encourages a holistic approach to instruction that allows children's social and academic competencies to be addressed simultaneously. Co-teaching teams of school psychologists and teachers integrate strategies for conflict resolution, self-regulation, and problem solving into content areas.

Teams of speech-language pathologists and teachers design and implement lessons, scaffolding language acquisition and pragmatics instruction into classroom literacy activities. Occupational therapists work with teachers to integrate sensory activities into classroom activities and routines. By partnering with colleagues to deliver instruction, teachers no longer feel alone with the trauma stories and traumatic reenactments of the children in their care. Instead, teachers process their feelings and remain objective through feedback and support from their co-teaching partners.

What Do You Think?

Mr. Giarrusso is co-teaching with Ms. Lucas, the school social worker. He is reluctant to let Ms. Lucas share instruction during the literacy block. He feels that he is the trained teacher. He does not mind if Ms. Lucas helps out individual children, but he does not believe that she should teach. What would you tell Mr. Giarrusso?

a   Try it for a while. You might be surprised at how much you enjoy having another adult in the room with you and how much Ms. Lucas can contribute.

b   Stick to a "one teach-one observe" model of co-teaching. Tell Ms. Lucas you will do the teaching while she observes.

c   If you have to have Ms. Lucas in the room, have her do social skills training with the children who need it. That's more in line with what she knows.

The correct answer is (a). Most teachers find that once they overcome their initial resistance to the idea, they enjoy having another adult in the room to work with. They find it invigorating to have someone available to share ideas with and brainstorm better ways of helping children succeed. Neither (b) nor (c) address the benefits of the co-teaching model for cross training and building the capacity of each teacher to teach all children.

Mental Health Supports for Teachers

Many researchers have written about the importance of collaboration between mental health and school professionals (Weist, Lowie,
Flaherty, & Pruitt, 2001). This type of collaborative partnership is
considered an essential support for staff attempting effective
instruction with at-risk populations (Bertacchi & Stott, 1989;
Brown & Thorpe, 1989; Shanok, 1989). The most helpful mental
health support focuses on services that relieve the stress felt by
teachers who are managing children's disruptive behavior (Ringeisen
et al., 2003). Trauma-specific in-service training and regularly
scheduled clinical consultation are particularly important.

Trauma-Specific Training

Preservice teacher training programs seldom prepare teachers for the
effects of trauma and violence on children's learning and development. As a result, teachers, are caught off guard by the life experiences of the children in their care. They need training focused on
how to infuse a trauma-sensitive approach into classroom activities
and routines. This includes ideas about avoiding the personalization
of children's behaviors, as well as how to intervene in ways that build
children's trust and independence. The support of trauma-specific
training helps teachers avoid the frustration of being unable to connect with children in meaningful ways. It helps them develop the
objectivity they need to remain emotionally responsive and focused
on developing children's competencies rather than engaging in endless cycles of conflict and trauma reenactments.

Clinical Consultation

Clinical consultation with a psychologist, psychiatrist, or clinical
social worker who is knowledgeable about the effects of trauma is
another effective way to help teachers recognize and guard against
symptoms of burnout or compassion fatigue (Koplow, 1996).
Regularly scheduled consultations give teachers a confidential
forum in which to explore and resolve feelings triggered by their
work with children (Garbarino et al., 1992). Consultation helps
teachers validate their feelings and identify the ways in which chil-

dren try to engage them in traumatic reenactments. Clinical consultation helps teachers recognize situations in which their assumptions about children's motivations or behaviors needs to change. It also helps teachers identify times when the pressure toward team consensus is keeping them from sharing observations or disagreeing with other team members.

Beth Anne's team contained great people. I particularly remember the outside psychologist who consulted with us once a month. She was always so willing to listen to whatever we had to say. Sometimes we'd spend the whole time venting our anger about a certain situation a child was in. Other times we complained about the children themselves, telling her how hard it was to be at the receiving end of rage all the time. And then, of course, there were the days we'd laugh like fools, just for the emotional release we felt after trying to contain our feelings all day long.

She was never judgmental. She'd let us have our say; then, she'd remind us it was important for us to have a place to talk about these feelings and let go of them rather than having them spill over into our own lives and families. She'd remind us of the need for clear boundaries and encourage us to take good care of ourselves.

I am really grateful my district provides this kind of support to us. My experience on that team really helped me understand how trauma effects not only children, but also the adults who work with them. It gave me confidence in my ability to help traumatized children. I feel good about the contribution I made to Beth Anne's life, as well as the many others who followed her.

What You Can Do

- Arrange for professional supervision with a mental health professional who is experienced in working with survivors of trauma and violence. Use supervision to acknowledge, express, and work through painful material with a supportive colleague.
- Learn more about the effects of trauma on children and those who care for them by logging on to web sites such as those sponsored the National Traumatic Stress Network (http://www.nctsnet.org). These federally funded research projects provide timely information on trauma-related topics. Other good sources of informa-

tion for teachers are the web sites http://www.schoolhousedoor.com and http://www.childtraumaacademy.org.

- Get on the mailing lists of national, state, and local organizations that advocate for children who are exposed to domestic or community violence. These organizations are a good source of information and training and provide a network of other professionals interested in protecting and caring for children exposed to violence.

- Shelters often provide community awareness training on the effects of violence against women and children. Ask your staff development coordinator to contact a local shelter for victims of domestic violence to schedule an in-service training.

What Do You Think?

Ms. Rivera works in a large urban school selected to participate in a collaborative partnership with a university-sponsored mental health program. University interns spend time in classrooms observing children's interactions with one another. In return, the university provides free clinical consultation to any teacher interested in participating. Ms. Rivera wants to participate but is afraid people will think she is incompetent if she does. What would you tell her?

a   Be careful. The principal might begin to suspect that your performance is lacking in some way if you decide to participate.

b   Do not let the consultant know how sad and angry you sometimes feel at the end of the day.

c   Use the time to learn more about how to engage traumatized children and respond to their needs.

The correct response is (c). Teachers who do not participate in programs that support their professional and emotional well-being are often overwhelmed by their reactions to children's behaviors or experiences. Participation in consultation sessions is a way of managing their own stress and learning more about trauma. Principals who are aware of the possible effects of trauma on teachers would be unlikely to question a teacher's professional performance for wanting to attend (a). The purpose of this type of consultation is to share feelings in a confidential setting. A teacher should have no qualms about letting his or her feelings be heard during consultation (b). Such consultation is used to acknowledge and validate teachers' emotional responses so that they are more able to acknowledge and respond to a broad range of children's emotional experiences and expressions.

CONCLUSION

Teachers are an invaluable resource to children exposed to violence or relational trauma. Their emotional availability and consistent presence help these children reestablish a sense of trust and learn to regulate their emotions and behavior. The intensity of this type of responsive teaching depletes a teacher's personal and professional resources. This demoralizes teachers and puts them at risk for burnout or compassion fatigue. Supports need to be in place to help teachers manage the emotional dimensions of their work and maintain their own sense of competence and well-being. These include a willingness to take the time necessary to protect one's own physical, emotional, and spiritual health; administrative support for collaborative teaming; and frequent opportunities for training.

8

Creating Trauma-Sensitive Schools

The sheer number of children exposed to some form of violence or abuse suggests that any program of educational reform must include plans for counteracting its traumatizing effects. Viewing all aspects of children's school experience through trauma-sensitive eyes is an important first step in creating a school culture that helps children move beyond the adversity in their lives. A trauma-sensitive approach helps educators appreciate the fact that many of the troublesome, intractable behaviors observed in their students are related to overwhelming experiences of violence and other forms of relational trauma. They are therefore better prepared to anticipate children's needs and facilitate the development of their social and academic competence. This chapter explores how to integrate a trauma-sensitive perspective into school climate, teacher–student relationships, and instructional practices.

Wesley is bigger and taller than most of the other fifth graders. His mother is really worried about him because the neighborhood they live in has some pretty nasty things going on in it. Last year, he had a lot of trouble and was eventually suspended for fighting. People are concerned that if he doesn't get turned around pretty soon, he might hurt somebody and wind up in real trouble.

I volunteered to have Wesley in my classroom. I can usually find a way to work with difficult children. I enjoy the challenge. And our school is committed to working as a team. I knew my colleagues would be there to support my efforts with Wesley. Together we'd find a way for him to succeed.

CHARACTERISTICS OF A TRAUMA-SENSITIVE SCHOOL CLIMATE

What You Know	You know that learning occurs most easily in safe, nurturing environments where children are encouraged to explore their interests and develop their potential.
What's New	A trauma-sensitive school climate is characterized by respect and supports capable of "taking over" when children's coping skills fail.

A trauma-sensitive school climate is one in which caring adults are committed to developing a school culture that can contain, manage, and help transform the life experiences of traumatized children. These schools serve as a protective environment for children, helping them acquire the social, emotional, and physical resources they need to succeed. They are nurturing, developmentally appropriate, and educationally rich environments that advocate for, support, and believe in all children (Garbarino et al., 1992).

At first I was a little put off by the idea of trauma-sensitive schools. I thought, "What else can they ask us to do?" But as the principal reminded me, "It's not like we don't have these children in school already. Learning more about how to reduce the effects of trauma will make it easier for us to give them what they need." He was right. Understanding how trauma affects children's learning and behavior has helped me appreciate the importance of safe and predictable classrooms in diminishing the impact of violence in other parts of the children's lives.

Building Children's Strengths

Trauma-sensitive schools move beyond traditional intervention models that focus on fixing or controlling behavior problems. They work with students to build their strengths. They encourage children to revise their explanatory narratives so that a belief in their capacity to exercise control over themselves and their environment exists. They provide children with easy access to supportive and powerful adults and opportunities to participate in decisions that affect their day-to-day functioning. These supports give children the flexibility they need to develop social and regulatory behaviors while continuing to make academic progress. In trauma-sensitive schools, staff members understand the core issues facing traumatized children. They understand as well the power of trauma to "stir the pot" and engage even experienced staff in patterns of reactive, crisis-driven behaviors. Trauma-sensitive schools take care to avoid coercive discipline while maintaining a focus on learning and instruction (Garbarino et al., 1992). They incorporate structures that help staff solve problems and support one another's efforts to remain empathic and in control.

Maintaining Safety

Creating a trauma-sensitive school culture requires a commitment to the safety of both children and staff. Many of the learning problems experienced by traumatized children flow from the persistent state of fear in which they live. Trapped in the past, they repeatedly replay their conflict and struggles in the present. Sometimes this includes angry, aggressive behaviors that threaten the safety of teachers and peers. Faced with repeated exposure to acting out behavior, teachers may lose confidence in their ability to make a difference in the lives of these fearful yet scary children. They give up on their efforts to build the regulatory capacity of these children and resort to coercive practices to maintain control (Farragher & Yanosy, 2005). As a result, the potential for using educational experiences to reduce the effects of trauma is lost. Knowing how to create a climate of positive behavior support (PBS), capable of "taking over" when children's coping ability fails, is therefore a critical step in maintaining the safety required for a trauma-sensitive school (Garbarino et al., 1992). Within this supportive context, children begin to repair the damage brought about by violence.

Providing Positive Behavior Support

Anticipating where and when problem behaviors are most likely to occur, trauma-sensitive schools use the framework of PBS to prevent them. This model is an extension of applied behavior analysis. It uses a lifestyle approach within natural settings to support children's efforts to demonstrate the behaviors they need to be successful (Turnbull, Edmonson, Griggs, Wickham, Sailor, Freeman, et al., 2002). This model is useful for trauma-sensitive schools because of its emphasis on consistency, the development of collaborative partnerships between staff and students, and the flexible nature of the support it provides.

The PBS model recognizes that there are common school problems that can be anticipated and planned for so that disruptions and conflict are minimized (Sugai, Horner, Dunlap, Hieneman, Lewis, Nelson, et al., 2000). It encourages school-based teams to use what they know about schools and the children who attend them to develop creative ways to prevent behaviors that are inconsistent with school success. A team approach is used to identify and define a limited number of behavioral expectations that children and staff work on together throughout the routines of the day. These expectations are clearly defined and consistently referred to. They are discussed, using a common language that reinforces the model's focus on anticipating and preventing problems. Universal supports—that is, supports that children need in order to meet agreed-upon expectations—are identified and provided across all school settings to all children.

Universal Supports

Universal supports include opportunities to understand what expected behaviors involve, direct instruction on the code of conduct required by each expectation, and schoolwide acknowledgment when children succeed at meeting the expectations. Feedback from children and observations of their performance at different times of the day, or in situations that vary in their complexity or stimulation, are part of the collaborative partnership. Data from both children and teachers are used to change environments and adjust levels of support to meet children's changing needs and monitor their successes.

Consistent use of universal supports helps schools eliminate most dangerous or threatening behaviors without resorting to punitive disciplinary practices. There are, however, some children whose behaviors continue to interfere with their ability to be successful in school. The PBS model recommends providing these children with more intensive support within their general education classroom to help them learn ways of getting their needs met in a manner consistent with the school's universal expectations. These additional supports scaffold onto classroom activities and routines and can be provided at either the individual or group level. For example, a child's efforts to control emotional outbursts are supported by the school psychologist's presence in the classroom during a class meeting when the child may receive feedback from peers or other predictably stressful times. Or, a group of children struggling to use language to express their thoughts and feelings are given the support of literacy activities that include explorations of feelings through text. These additional supports are monitored regularly and remain in place until the children requiring them are able to meet behavioral expectations by relying only on universal supports.

What You Can Do

- Talk with your supervisor to determine how a schoolwide decision can be made regarding a set of ground rules used to guide student behaviors.
- Talk with your supervisor to determine how a schoolwide decision can be made regarding the universal supports made available to children throughout the day. These may include making staff available to greet children as they get off the bus; adopting block scheduling to reduce transitions; building opportunities for physical movement and stress reduction into classroom activities and routines; creating visual templates that sequence the steps in routine tasks; and using class meetings to air disagreements, solve problems, and hone friendship skills.
- Review student records to identify activities or times of day that are particularly stressful for individual children. Consider changing performance expectations or providing additional support to help the child successfully cope with these situations. Meet with individual children to identify the goals that they want to focus on.

- Work with individual students to develop a plan for reaching each goal, agree on indicators of progress toward achieving it, and schedule times to check in with one another to evaluate how things are going.

What Do You Think?

Mr. Gonzalez is the principal of a middle school where many of the students have aggressive, acting out behaviors. He wants to institute the positive behavior support model but is concerned that teachers will not be able to control the children's behavior without the use of negative consequences. What would you tell him?

a By the time they get to middle school, children need to know that aggressive, acting out behaviors will not be tolerated. Clear consequences, such as suspension and failing grades, are the only way to get students to comply and do what they are told to do.

b Consistent use of PBS helps children learn to control their emotions and regulate their behavior in ways that allow them to participate successfully in school.

c School needs to prepare children for real life. No one gets PBS in the workplace. You are told what to do, and if you refuse, you get fired.

The correct answer is (b). When PBS is provided in a consistent and collaborative manner, even children who act out or behave aggressively are given the safety and support they need to control their emotions and behavior. Threats of consequences or suspension (a) often reinforce children's distorted perceptions of themselves and increase their stress levels rather than producing any real change in behavior. Although it is true that children need to know how to conduct themselves appropriately at work to avoid getting fired (c), the best way to teach those behaviors is by rehearsing and practicing them with a trusted adult.

Our school is committed to using PBS. It just makes so much sense to anticipate and plan for times when children may need more support rather than reacting to situations that could be avoided. It feels good to help children learn to take responsibility for their behavior—identifying when they need extra attention or support instead of just demanding compliance from them.

I think the hardest part for our staff was agreeing on the specifics of working with the children to address certain behaviors so that we could provide the consistency the students needed. We didn't want one teacher letting the children wear hats and another making students take them off. We spent several staff meetings deciding on which behaviors are nonnegotiable, which can be resolved collaboratively with children, and which are best ignored.

It was pretty easy to decide on a set of safety guidelines that would be enforced throughout the school. The staff agreed to redirect children and provide additional support whenever one of the guidelines appeared on the verge of being broken. Next, we listed behaviors that are best ignored. This was harder because none of us wanted to let go of our pet peeves, but we didn't want to overwhelm the children. We knew that it would be hard to ensure consistency if we tried to intervene in too many behaviors, so we agreed to limit interventions to goals that could benefit all of the children, such as getting to activities on time, asking for help, and cooperating with others. We talked to the children about these behaviors and worked with them to describe what each behavior would look like and sound like at our school.

Then, we were ready to target behaviors to work on with individual children. Instead of thinking, "I want Wesley to stop swearing," we needed to identify what we wanted him to do—use appropriate language to express frustration, get help before frustration set in. We involved the children in setting these goals, asking them which behaviors they were most interested in focusing on. We identified the supports they would need to meet these targets. Could they succeed with only universal support, or did they need something more intensive? We worked with individual students to develop their strengths rather than focus on their weaknesses.

The results are amazing. Our students are able to tell us when they have done something well. They are beginning to anticipate when situations might be difficult for them and ask for support to get through them. There are fewer incidents of acting out behavior and more overtures of friendship and support.

Creating a Positive Peer Culture

Children exposed to violence are often more isolated than their peers (Pynoos, Steinburg, & Goenjian, 1996). Fears of community violence or unrealistic expectations held by parents limit their opportunities to play with other children and interact socially. As a result, children who have experienced trauma fail to acquire many of the social skills learned in this context (Piaget, 1932). Role taking is difficult, as is the ability to discriminate among different types of relationships and the rules that define interactions within them (Oden, 1988). This lack of social competence, coupled with children's observations of adults using force to solve problems, makes them particularly vulnerable to bullying behaviors, either as the aggressor or the victim (Shields & Cicchetti, 2001). In either case, their behavior signals an inability to form mutually satisfying relationships with others and poses a safety threat to them or their peers.

Trauma-sensitive schools take active measures to prevent bullying in all its forms. The code of conduct in these schools includes a commitment to nonviolence and the maintenance of a school climate where children feel cared for and secure (Hawkins, Guo, Hill, Battin-Pearson, & Abbott, 1996). Opportunities for children to experience connections between themselves and caring adults are built into everyday activities and routines. Cooperative games and project-based instruction develop collaboration and friendship skills.

Behavior management focuses on self-regulation rather than compliance. Direct instruction in skills necessary for successful conflict resolution reduces disruptive behavior and promotes problem solving and compromise. Within the context of this supportive environment, children acquire the skills they need to relate to one another in safe, supportive ways.

What Do You Think?

Ms. McMahon teaches at an elementary school located in an urban neighborhood known for its poverty and violent gang activity. She gets frustrated when some of her students egg one another on to act in hurtful, negative ways. Ms. McMahon is looking for ways to help the children learn to treat people with more care and respect but is not sure what to do. What would you tell her?

a   Ignore the behavior as much as possible. Encourage the class to avoid interactions with students who tease or make fun of others.

b   Work with other staff members to create a school climate where acts of kindness and support are noticed and described in terms of strength and maturity.

c   Limit opportunities for peer interactions. Assign troublesome children escorts to accompany them while walking in the hallways and to the bus. Tell these students that they have to earn the right to be part of the classroom by demonstrating appropriate behaviors.

The correct answer is (b). Ignoring hurtful behaviors (a) or isolating children who exhibit them (c) does nothing to address the destructive nature of these negative behaviors. Children become more respectful of and helpful to one another in environments where these model behaviors are acknowledged by adults and defined as exemplifying status and maturity.

Promoting Self-Care

Exposure to violence and other forms of relational trauma interferes with children's ability to use good judgment in assessing the danger inherent in some of their behaviors. Cognitive distortions that help them explain or excuse the behavior of irresponsible or dangerous caregivers may lead them to minimize the effects of other harmful behaviors. These children are prone to repetitive involvement in exploitative or dangerous relationships (Herman, 1992). Because they are unable to use other people as a source of help and support, they often make poor choices about how to handle the stress that they endure on a regular basis. Some use drugs or alcohol to regulate out-of-control thoughts and emotions (Felitti, Anda, Nordenberg, Williamson, Spitz, Edwards, et al., 1998). Many engage in high-risk or high-intensity behaviors in an effort to connect emotionally and escape intolerable feelings of despair and isolation (Dayton, 2000). The stress associated with family violence causes some children to crave the intense sensation of self-inflicted pain to regain control of their body. Some actually cut themselves, whereas others may bite themselves or dig at scabs or cuts (Herman, 1992).

The people who staff trauma-sensitive schools are trained to look beyond these defensive behaviors to the underlying issues that give rise to them. They recognize that traumatized children can be a danger to themselves. They diligently work with mental health collaborators to support children in taking responsibility for their own safety and well-being. Wellness programs teach children stress management techniques and give them opportunities to experience other people as sources of comfort and protection rather than harm. These programs teach children how to be self-protective, helping students plan activities that promote health and well-being and avoid situations that can lead to self-injurious behavior.

What You Can Do

- Ask staff members to draft a safety plan that lists the steps they will take when they find themselves in stressful, dangerous, or challenging situations. Encourage them to use their plans to help children design and use their own.

- Commit to creating a crisis-free classroom. Eliminate terms such as *crisis intervention* or *crisis counselor.* Instead, encourage children to work with you to anticipate problems and create solutions and options for additional support before situations get out of control.

- Notice, acknowledge, and actively elicit acts of kindness.

- Actively intervene to stop stereotyping and teasing.

DE-ESCALATING BEHAVIOR

What You Know	You know that schools play an important role in helping children learn to control their behavior and engage in positive interactions with peers.
What's New	Children exposed to violence often need adult support to learn how to de-escalate to manage emotions and behavior. They need encouragement to interact with peers in a mutually satisfying manner.

Traumatized children have a hard time trusting teachers and other authority figures because early attachment experiences have trapped them in a "seemingly endless feedback loop of destructive repetition" (Bloom, 2005, p. 9). As noted in Chapter 5, these children are quick to engage staff in interactions that mimic their primary attachment experiences. Something in the interaction, perhaps a facial expression or tone of voice, signals threat or danger, even though the current context is not dangerous at all. The children react with self-defeating patterns of behavior that trigger cycles of unnecessary conflict between themselves and their teachers. This pattern of traumatic reenactment seriously limits children's ability to collaborate with adults to improve their life circumstances. The staff members of trauma-sensitive schools are trained to recognize these reactions as symptomatic of the original trauma. They avoid responding in a manner that further escalates the conflict or inadvertently retraumatizes a child. Instead, they react in a manner that helps the child de-escalate his or her behavior and move on.

The process of de-escalating behavior with a caring adult provides traumatized children with support in learning how to regulate their emotions and behavior. Like the coregulation experienced by many children in their early attachment relationships, the de-escalation process relies on the adult's own capacity for self-regulation to help a child acquire the control that he or she needs. It is a powerful tool for helping children learn to recognize what triggers their destructive behaviors. The process helps children correct the cognitive distortions that fuel conflicts with staff while providing a language to describe disturbing or intolerable inner states.

I used to work in a residential school where I learned some strategies that help children de-escalate their behaviors. They have been pretty easy to integrate into a general education classroom, so I've been using them for years as part of my behavior management system. I thought they might help Wesley, so I agreed to have him in my class.

The first few days were rough. He kept trying to engage me in a power struggle, but I refused to get caught. Instead, I encouraged him to tell me what he was thinking when he started acting out. It didn't take long to realize that he thought everyone was out to get him and that it was only a matter of time before he'd get kicked out. He felt totally powerless to change what was going on. I suggested ways he could start to take more control over what happened to him. We made a deal that he would put a red card on his desk when he felt like he was losing control. That would be my signal to give him some support, by either giving him a break or a few minutes to check in with me. He agreed to try, and over the last few months his acting out behaviors have decreased. I have learned to anticipate when he needs more support and build it into my lesson plans for the day. But it's not easy.

De-escalation starts with giving a child an opportunity to describe the disrupting event from his or her point of view. The child is encouraged to establish a time line for the disturbing incident, listing the steps that led up to the current conflict or problem (Brendtro & Larson, 2006; LaVoie, 1994; Long & Dufner, 1980). The adult's role is to *listen* and accept the child's interpretation while introducing alternatives to the child's thinking and behavior. The child is encouraged to identify how he or she was feeling at the time of the incident, if necessary using vocabulary provided by the adult. As the child calms down, he or she discusses with the adult the outcomes of the behavior and decide what measures to take to prevent the conflict from recurring. When appropriate, the adult supports the child's efforts to repair any damage resulting from the conflict.

What You Can Do

- Partner with a school psychologist or social worker to learn how to de-escalate the acting out behaviors of children caught in a conflict cycle.
- Teach children about the conflict cycle. Analyze the behavior of characters in favorite stories by using the steps followed to de-escalate conflict.
- Use team meetings or conversations with a supervisor to talk about any counter-aggressive feelings you may be having toward children in your care. These feelings are a normal part of working with traumatized children, but unless they are addressed, they can interfere with your ability to help the students de-escalate their behavior.
- Read stories from multiple perspectives. Help children see that the private logic of one character is not the only way of interpreting the events taking place.
- Use writing assignments that ask children to respond to the events in a story from the point of view of one character. Discuss the different perspectives, noting the similarities and differences in interpretation and how the character's interpretation of events informs his or her behavior.

BUILDING SOCIAL COMPETENCE THROUGH PEER INTERACTIONS AND SERVICE

What You Know	You know that school plays an important role in helping children acquire age-appropriate social skills.
What's New	Children traumatized by family violence may need additional support to play and participate with peers.

Trauma-sensitive schools buffer the effects of violence and relational trauma by helping children manage their reactions to the challenging circumstances of their lives. The schools do this by creating learning environments that recognize the importance of friendship, play, and service in developing children's social competence. They nurture classroom communities where all children are included in meaningful and respectful ways.

Wesley didn't really know how to be around other children. He wasn't comfortable with them. He didn't know how to play many of the games they enjoyed and often misunderstood their jokes. During recess and free time, he kept pretty much to himself. His efforts to join in were awkward and sometimes interpreted by the other children as aggression.

I started introducing organized games or craft activities at recess. I'd invite Wesley and some of the other children to join me on a rotating basis. I used the time we were playing together to model social skills and mediate a relationship between Wesley and the other children. I'd mention things that I knew he and the other children had in common or were interested in. When it seemed that Wesley and the other children could sustain a conversation on their own, I moved to another group.

I think these mediated play times gave Wesley and the other children an opportunity to get to know one another a little bit better. Over time, Wesley learned to approach children in a more appropriate, caring way. Some of the children started to include him at lunch and recess. They seem to feel less intimidated by him and to be more willing to give him a chance.

Social Competence

Social competence is the capacity to effectively manage social situations and engage in mutually satisfying relationships with others. Social competence includes the ability to use social language and behavior to form friendships and deal effectively with diverse social situations. It develops most easily when children have frequent opportunities to interact and play with other children. These peer interactions help children develop the social skills and emotional intelligence they need to form friendships, resolve conflicts, make use of important social information, and make meaningful contributions to others.

Friendship

Children exposed to violence often find themselves excluded from the friendship circle of their peers (Feerick & Silverman, 2006). Some children are left out of the group because other children view their aggressive behavior as threatening or out of control. These children react to others in an impulsive manner that suggests a "strike first" posture in response to any perception of peer hostility (Cole et al., 2005). They lack insight into how their behavior affects other children, often seeing peers as sources of pleasure or terror but seldom as fellow humans (van der Kolk, 2005).

Other children have deep feelings of shame, making it difficult for them to reach out to peers or engage in everyday conversation. Fear of disclosing family secrets make these children act in ways that peers label as deviant or weird (Pynoos, Steinburg, & Goenjian, 1996). They appear apathetic and socially withdrawn and somewhat indifferent to other children (Brazelton & Greenspan, 2001). Their style of play is often repetitive and boring to peers. They seldom initiate interactions and do not respond easily to other children's bids to play. As a result, they are viewed as socially inept and are seldom included games or activities (Feldman, Salzinger, Rosario, & Alvardo, 1995).

Limited play experiences further exacerbate the social isolation experienced by many children exposed to violence. As discussed previously, neighborhood safety concerns may limit their opportunities for social activity and outside play (Fantuzzo, 1991), and excessive responsibilities or parental expectations may keep these children from after-school activities such as team sports or social clubs. Burdened with protecting younger siblings or bearing the emotional burden of a parent's pain leave these children ill equipped to move easily into the social world of children their own age. As a result, the children often lack the skills needed to engage in the games and leisure time activities that form the basis for friendships among school-age children (Cooper, 2000).

Wesley doesn't have any real friends. He's quick to pick fights or go off in a huff if he thinks one of the other children is looking at him funny or judging him somehow. On the playground, he kind of wanders around, watching the other children or playing by himself. If he tries to join a game, he does it in such disruptive ways that the other children are put off by him.

The school psychologist has been working with Wesley and some of the other boys. She is teaching them how to play simple games like catch or pickup basketball, things you think he'd already know how to do. We play board games at indoor recess—anything to help him experience the give and take that goes with play and relationships. I'm even bringing in baseball scores and information about the players, trying to help him have something to talk about with the other children.

Trauma-sensitive schools provide instruction on how to be a friend, as well how to manage conflict and repair misunderstandings as they happen. Shared projects, simulations, and team-based assignments help children learn how to sustain social interaction and experience the reciprocity that is often absent in other parts of their lives. They provide a context for building children's capacity to project an image of themselves that others are attracted to and respect (Levine, 2002a). Through these activities, children learn how to approach peers in a cooperative and thoughtful manner that fosters acceptance and a sense of belonging.

Conflict Resolution

Children exposed to violence often share a cognitive profile that makes conflict resolution difficult for them. As discussed in Chapter 2, a lack of consistent interactions with primary attachment figures results in a fairly inflexible cognitive style that makes it difficult to generate alternative solutions to problems. Deficits in the area of language pragmatics or social language reduce these students' effectiveness in negotiating with peers. This situation, coupled with a limited understanding of cause and effect, leads to poor frustration tolerance and a tendency to give up or withdraw. As a result, these children often exhibit behaviors that are maladaptive for success in social interactions. For example, as explained in Chapter 3, they may have meltdowns or erupt in anger when the cognitive demands of the situation exceed their capacity to respond adaptively (Greene, 2001).

Trauma-sensitive schools provide children with opportunities to acquire the skills they need for to resolve conflicts effectively. The de-escalation strategies previously discussed in this chapter give children an opportunity to work with a caring adult to correct the cognitive distortions that limit their ability to negotiate with peers. These students develop social language fluency by talking with teachers about feelings and words to express them, as well as by frequently working in groups with peers. When appropriate, children are encouraged to use scripted language in situations where they feel particularly vulnerable or anxious. Direct instruction is provided in how to ask questions or request clarifications in a socially appropriate manner. Classroom meetings, facilitated by thoughtful adults, teach children how to focus on solving problems rather than attributing blame or seeking retaliation. With enough practice, students learn view one another as partners in search of a fair solution to a problem rather than adversaries locked in unchangeable conflict (Gregg, 1998).

Using Social Information

Chapter 3 discussed how exposure to violence interferes with social cognition—that is, the ability to arrive at accurate interpretations of social events and expectations. Children exposed to violence often appear socially awkward—unable to engage in spontaneous, informal conversations or play (Howard, 1986). Heightened perceptions of negativity or danger lead to misunderstandings and unnecessary confrontations (Dodge, Pettit, Bates, & Valente, 1995). Past experiences with unpredictable or dangerous adults cloud interactions with teachers, often leading to power struggles or patterns of noncompliance (Craig, 1992).

Trauma-sensitive schools provide children with opportunities to become more socially aware. For instance, teams of teachers and children observe social situations, identifying the communication patterns that are characteristic of peer interactions and adult–child interactions. Direct instruction is provided in how to use language to delay impulsive reactions to possible threats or negativity. Class meetings and group activities are used to practice asking clarifying questions and using feedback to correct misperceptions.

These schools place particular emphasis on helping children understand the role that rules play in enabling them to them stay safe and in control. The children are encouraged to work with teachers and classmates to develop and follow rules that serve a specific purpose. For example, a rule that requires students to walk in the hallways prevents children from falling or tripping. A rule that calls for students to use "inside voices" for group work helps children hear what other people in their group are saying. Some children may benefit from adopting personal rules that help them interact more successfully with peers—for example, refusing to think about home so they can pay attention to what the people around them are saying or counting to 10 before acting on feelings of aggression or anger.

As children become better able to anticipate what is expected in different social situations, they can participate more successfully. They learn to check their interpretation of events against the observations of others. They also learn that rules can protect their best interests and help them achieve personal goals. Finally, they learn that some adults are on their side, ready to help them successfully adapt to the challenges of their lives.

What You Can Do

- Model and explain the prosocial behaviors required in different situations. Talk about how different types of relationships require different ways of interacting. Coach children in how to interpret various social situations and how to adjust their behavior to meet expectations.

- Prioritize social behaviors, working on them one at a time. Encourage children to support one another's efforts to acquire a targeted skill. Celebrate progress and success.

- Serve lunch and snack family style to foster close adult–child interaction and model appropriate social behaviors.
- Teach children how to play age-appropriate games. Provide opportunities for students to learn the rules of and practice playing popular sports.
- Give children basic social information about their school and community, including available extracurricular activities, common neighborhood events, and the history of where they live.
- Keep up with the culture of your students' age group. Know about the books, music, and media they enjoy, as well activities in which they are interested.

What Do You Think?

Jenny is a student in Ms. Peters' second-grade class. The other children avoid Jenny, leaving her out of games and outside activities. Ms. Peters thinks this is because Jenny never speaks to any of the children; she spends her free time reading or drawing by herself. Ms. Peters wants to help Jenny connect more to her peers. What would you tell Ms. Peters to do?

a Let Jenny be. Some children like to be alone. She should not be required to play with other children if she does not want to. Maybe she has nothing in common with them.

b Tell Jenny that she cannot take a book or drawing materials to recess. Assign her to a group activity such as hopscotch or foursquare. Keep encouraging Jenny to play until she participates like everyone else.

c Invite Jenny and another child to play a game with you during recess or free time. As you play the game, facilitate a conversation between Jenny and the other child. Continue to offer Jenny this type of support until she is comfortable playing with the other child by herself.

The correct answer is (c). Jenny needs the support of a caring adult to help her connect with peers. Teaching Jenny to play a game that other children enjoy while facilitating a conversation between her and another child gives Jenny an opportunity to acquire the play skills she needs to feel comfortable with peers. Leaving her alone (a) or forcing her into activities without support or instruction in how to play (b) would do little to teach Jenny social skills and may make her more vulnerable to teasing or rejection by peers.

Meaningful Service to Others

Trauma-sensitive schools move beyond simply providing services to children. They provide opportunities for students to give meaningful service to others. Service learning taps into children's altruism, making them more aware of their ability to respond to others in caring, respectful ways. It helps mobilize their inner resources to turn toward the future, trying out new roles and practicing new behaviors (Bloom, 2005). In addition, service learning fosters students' sense of purpose and personal efficacy as they observe the impact of their good deeds on other people's lives.

As I got to know Wesley, I realized he had lots of strengths that weren't being tapped into at school. He told me one day that he really liked going to see his grandmother on the weekends. She lives in an assisted living center in the neighborhood. He goes there every Saturday and plays cards with her.

Wesley's story about his grandmother gave me the idea of finding places where Wesley could develop his compassionate, kind side. I asked a friend who coaches Special Olympics if Wesley could help out. At first she was a little taken aback by the idea, given Wesley's reputation, but she agreed to give it a try. Wesley was assigned to help Tyler, a boy who has Muscular Dystrophy. It's a progressive disease, and Tyler is in the last stages of it. He can't walk, and his speech is hard to understand.

Well, you should see what Tyler has done for Wesley! He has taught Wesley that Wesley matters. When Tyler sees Wesley, his face lights up and he smiles from ear to ear. Wesley thinks about Tyler a lot, trying to come up with ways to keep him actively involved in the games. He looks for jokes that Tyler will enjoy and seems really pleased when Tyler laughs. To the outsider it looks like Wesley is helping Tyler. But to us in the know, Tyler is helping Wesley grow past his hard beginnings. He's helping Wesley define himself as someone who cares—someone who can make a difference.

What You Can Do

- Conduct talent hunts to help children identify hidden strengths (Brendtro & Larson, 2006).

- Organize a Big Brother Big Sister program in your school. Partner students in primary and intermediate classrooms to provide mentoring, services, and support to one another.
- Integrate service learning experiences into the curriculum. For example, have children gather oral histories of residents at a local long-term care facility. This type of interviewing helps children make connections with older people while enriching their understanding of the history of the local community (Brendtro & Larson, 2006).
- Collaborate with community service programs such as the Society for the Prevention of Cruelty to Animals (SPCA) to link children to age-appropriate service opportunities in the neighborhood.

What Do You Think?

Ms. Huber teaches fifth grade. She knows that two of her students have been in and out of foster care. She knows that the mother of a third child has recently taken out a restraining order against her husband. She has read that children exposed to violence can benefit from service learning but is not sure what this would look like in an elementary classroom. What would you tell Ms. Huber?

a   Partner with the kindergarten classroom in your building. Arrange for children from your classroom to be Big Brothers and Big Sisters to the younger children. Schedule times during the week when your students can read to the kindergarten children, help them with projects, or play with them during recess or free time.

b   Fifth grade is pretty young for children to do service learning. Assign them reading projects that tell about how community workers such as firefighters, first responders, and doctors serve others, but do not involve the students in any service projects.

c   The children you are worried about are under a lot of stress. Do not add to their problems by asking them to be responsible for other children. They can barely manage being responsible for themselves.

The correct answer is (a). As long as the service in which the children are involved is age appropriate and within their developmental capacity, it is a great way to build self-confidence. Reading about community helpers (b) does not give children the same sense of meaning and personal fulfillment that service learning does. Rather than increasing children's stress (c), age-appropriate service learning can help children learn that they have something to contribute, that they are of value.

BUILDING COMPETENCE THROUGH CONSISTENT USE OF INSTRUCTIONAL BEST PRACTICES

What You Know	You know that children learn best when instruction involving personal interests is used to motivate students to explore essential concepts. Ongoing assessment and self-reflection help children acquire critical thinking skills as they master content.
What's New	Best practices, such as those included within the differentiated instruction model, provide teachers with an instructional framework that is flexible enough to address the social and academic needs of children exposed to violence within the context of school activities and routines.

Trauma-sensitive schools recognize that children's academic competence depends on educational experiences that are responsive to their unique needs. Structures need to be in place to correct persistent cognitive distortions; limit reactive, impulsive behaviors; and, at the same time, provide access to a meaningful curriculum. Differentiated instruction is an example of a teaching framework flexible enough to address the specific needs of these children while adhering to high academic standards.

Differentiated Instruction

The differentiated instruction model anticipates that individual differences exist within any group of children; therefore, planning occurs with that diversity in mind (Tomlinson, 2001). All children learn about essential concepts but at different levels of complexity and with varying levels of support, as needed (Tomlinson, & Eidson, 2003). Children's interests and strengths guide the design of instruction and are repeatedly addressed within the structures used to support personal growth and academic progress. These structures include planning by concept, using ongoing assessment, implementing flexible grouping, encouraging choice making, and fostering self-reflection.

Planning by Concept

Differentiated instruction uses core concepts and key principles to organize curriculum content. Concepts such as cause and effect are explained and applied across content areas, helping children acquire a broader conceptual understanding of the world. Children are encouraged to take the roles of experts or real people and solve authentic problems that are related to the concepts they are studying. Important skills, such as learning to follow a sequence of problem-solving steps, are embedded within playful, creative activities that keep children motivated and involved.

Repeated opportunities to work with concepts via differentiated instruction help children correct many of the conceptual problems discussed in Chapter 2. They learn to consider experiences from a variety of perspectives. Rules of private logic expand to include alternative points of view. Incidents of self-defeating behavior decrease as children use their improved understanding of cause and effect to identify better ways to manage their behavior and emotions. Self-centered thinking gives way to empathic understanding as children explore the emotions related to the roles they play in classroom simulations.

Using Ongoing Assessment

Differentiated instruction uses ongoing assessment of children's knowledge, understanding, and skills to create educational experiences that reflect who they are as learners. Assessments of children's preferences and interests inform the content of instruction, as well as the selection of classroom activities and the products used to demonstrate their learning. Children actively participate in their own learning by selecting projects or tasks that reflect their interests and learning profiles. Teachers work collaboratively with children to monitor their progress toward meaningful instructional goals. They provide a variety of ways for children to demonstrate what they have learned and tell students early on the criteria that will be used to evaluate their performance.

The teacher–student relationship that is encouraged within this assessment process can be thought of as a type of attachment relationship, in which adult skills and knowledge facilitate and support child growth and development. Teachers change what they do to ensure children's success; they encourage children to develop their own interests and points of view; and they serve as attuned observers of children's behaviors, helping students reach personal goals and engage in meaningful work.

At the beginning of the school year, Wesley was always telling me how much he hated school. He said it was boring. He complained about all the "baby work" teachers wanted him to do. As far as he was concerned, it was all stupid.

That was my opening. I asked him what kind of work would he rather do. What kind of things interested him? What could he do in school that would be meaningful to him? It was the beginning of an ongoing hunt to help Wesley and I discover his talents. I was glad that he was letting me help.

At first we had these conversations in private, usually during our weekly teacher–student conference time. But as Wesley became more confident and began to trust me more, he was able to become an active participant in the self-assessments that I build into my teaching. He got better at knowing the kinds of activities that were best for him; he's a kinesthetic learner, so he really enjoys using projects to "show what he knows."

It has also been good for Wesley to work with other students. He's much more willing to share and help out than he was in the beginning of the year. He hasn't said that he hates school in a really long time.

Implementing Flexible Grouping

Differentiated instruction uses flexible grouping to give children opportunities to work with a wide variety of classmates and in a wide range of contexts throughout the day. Groups are organized around specific goals of instruction, so some groups are interest driven, whereas others focus on similar levels of skill readiness. Sometimes children are grouped with peers who have similar learning styles; at other times, children with different learning styles work together to complete a task that requires a variety of skills. Flexible grouping recognizes the social benefits of learning to work with different people in meaningful and productive ways, as well as the cognitive benefits derived from approaching problems from multiple perspectives.

Flexible grouping is an excellent way to provide children with opportunities to shift between higher and lower levels of skill development or academic competence. Groups are organized in a manner that is consistent with a trauma-sensitive approach. Attention is given to developing children's strengths, as well as addressing skills and competencies yet to be acquired. The fluid membership of the groups prevents labeling children on the basis of a limited number of characteristics and underscores the variety of interests and skills within any group of children. Children are encouraged to try out new roles and new ways of relating as they rotate through groups. This builds their social competence and self-esteem while promoting an atmosphere of acceptance and belonging.

Encouraging Choice Making

Differentiated instruction recognizes the relationship between choice making and children's development of personal agency and decision-making skills. Choice making is built into all aspects of instruction: the tools children use to acquire the knowledge they need, the applications children select to improve their understanding of what they are learning, and the assessments used to evaluate their level of mastery. Children are encouraged to review their choices and determine their effectiveness in achieving personal goals.

Within this framework, choice making helps children who have been exposed to violence acquire a better understanding of cause-and-effect relationships and the influence that behavior can have on determining their goal achievement. The ability to reflect on the choices they have made, sometimes changing their original choice, encourages cognitive flexibility and higher order thinking.

Fostering Self-Reflection

Differentiated instruction helps children acquire a "vocabulary of thinking" and a structure to "think about thinking." Process logs and "thinking maps" are used to help children keep track of their thinking as they solve problems and complete tasks. These strategies train children to observe how they think—to note "the kind of thinking an instance calls for and the thinking process they use to make this decision" (Tomlinson & Eidson, 2003, p. 188). Teachers review these process logs to gain insight into how children set goals and monitor their progress toward achieving them.

For children exposed to violence, direct instruction on how to think about thinking promotes mindfulness. The students learn to direct their attention toward the thoughts that shape their behavior. This facilitates the development of the problem-solving skills associated with academic success and provides the children with a powerful tool for regulating their behavior. As teachers gain insight into how children think, they are able to work with students to correct cognitive distortions that interfere with feelings of competency and self-control.

What You Can Do

- Learn more about the concepts that spiral through the curricula you are using. Some state standards are organized by concept. Get in the habit of deciding the concept you want to address as the first step in lesson planning.
- Talk to children about the concepts they are learning. Encourage other teachers on your team to use the same language to describe a particular concept across content areas. This strategy helps children who have trouble with selection control know immediately where they need to focus their attention.

- Before designing a unit of instruction, assess children's knowledge of the subject area. Poll them to find out activities they would like to use to learn about the new topic. Use this assessment information to plan your lessons.

- Start each lesson with an activating activity that taps prior knowledge. Leave time at the end of each lesson for children to reflect on what they have learned. Repeated opportunities to reflect build children's capacity to monitor how they think and how they behave.

- When planning lessons, distinguish between assessment and evaluation. Assessment involves a collaborative partnership between teachers and children that is aimed at designing meaningful and responsive instruction. Evaluation involves the tasks used to determine which concepts children are able to apply correctly upon completion of a course of study.

- Incorporate decisions about flexible grouping into your lesson planning process. Make sure each child rotates among several different groups throughout the day.

What Do You Think?

Ms. Johnson recently attended a workshop on differentiated instruction. She thinks it is a great model and wants to use it with her students right away. She is concerned, however, that she will not be able to cover the entire curriculum if she gives children so much time to work in groups and reflect on what they have learned. What would you tell Ms. Johnson?

a   Planning for differentiated instruction is organized around core concepts that wind through all of the content areas. If you align your instruction with those core concepts, you will be able to cover the essential elements of the content areas in a manner that helps children integrate what they are learning.

b   You are right. Despite its benefits for children, differentiated instruction takes a lot of time and preparation. It is better to cover the basics by using a traditional instructional model and to use differentiated lessons for review.

c   Children have to be really mature to handle the group interaction involved in differentiated instruction. It would be very hard to use the model with children who act out and have below grade level skills.

The correct answer is (a). The collaboration and group processing involved in differentiated instruction helps children become more efficient and accurate learners. Although differentiated instruction does take a lot of planning (b), it helps students integrate what they are learning into meaningful patterns. Contrary to the opinion expressed in answer (c), differentiated instruction actually provides children with opportunities to learn both the interactive and academic skills that they need to be successful.

CONCLUSION

Trauma-sensitive schools scaffold information about trauma onto already-established best teaching practices. Staff members work in teams to create a blend of services, supports, and opportunities that is sensitive to individual needs while maintaining high standards of academic and social performance. Emphasis is placed on helping children gain access to and use available resources so that family or community violence does not undermine educational success (Cole et al., 2005). Trauma-sensitive schools do not replace learning with discipline (Garbarino et al., 1992). Rather, they use personal relationships and responsive teaching to nurture children's inherent capacity for self-control while developing their potential for academic and social competency.

References

Adelman, H.S., & Taylor, L. (2000). Moving prevention from the fringes into the fabric of school improvement. *Journal of Educational and Psychological Consultation, 11,* 7–36.

Adelman, H.S., & Taylor, L. (2003). On sustainability of project innovations as systemic change. *Journal of Educational and Psychological Consultation, 14,* 1–25.

Adler, J. (1994, January 10). Kids growing up scared. *Newsweek, 73,* 43–49.

Ainsworth, M.D.S., Blehar, M., Waters, E., & Wall, S. (1979). *Patterns of attachment: A psychological study of the strange situation.* Mahwah, NJ: Lawrence Erlbaum Associates.

Alvermann, D. (2005). Exemplary literacy instruction in grades 7–12: What counts and who's counting. In J. Flood & P. Anders (Eds.), *Literacy development of students in urban schools: Research and policy* (pp. 187–201). Newark, DE: International Reading Association.

Arnold, D.H. (1997). Co-occurrence of externalizing behavior problems and emergent academic difficulties in high-risk boys: A preliminary evaluation of patterns and mechanisms. *Applied Developmental Psychology, 18,* 317–330.

Axford, B. (2007). Children working together: A scaffolding literacy case study. *The Australian Journal of Language and Literacy, 30*(1), 21–39.

Banks, A. (2001). PTSD: *Relationships and brain chemistry.* Wellesley, MA: Stone Center Publications.

Bauer, R.H. (1987). Control processes as a way of understanding, diagnosing, and remediating learning disabilities. *Advances in Learning and Behavioral Disabilities, 2,* 41–81.

Belcastro, P.A., & Gold, R.S. (1983). Teacher stress and burnout: Implications for school health personnel. *Journal of School Health, 53,* 125–139.

Bentovim, A. (1992). *Trauma organizes systems.* London: Karnac Books.

Bergin, C. (2001). The parent–child relationship during beginning reading. *Journal of Literacy Research 33*(4), 681–706.

Bertacchi, J., & Stott, F.M. (1989). A seminar for supervisors in infant/family programs: Growing versus paying more for staying the same. In E. Fenichel (Ed.), *Learning through supervision and mentorship to support the development of infants, toddlers, and their families: A source book* (pp. 132–140). Washington, DC: ZERO TO THREE.

Bibou, N.I., Stogiannidou, A., & Klosseoglou, G. (1999). The relationship between teacher burnout and teachers' attributions and practices regarding school behavior problems. *School Psychology International, 20,* 209–217.

Blair, C. (2002). School readiness: Integrating cognition and emotion in a neuro-biological conceptualization of child functioning at school entry. *American Psychologist, 57*(2), 111–127.

Bloom, S. (2005). The sanctuary model of organizational change for children's residential treatment. *International Journal for Therapeutic and Supportive Organizations, 26*(1), 65–81.

Botvin, G., Schinke, S., Epstein, J., Diaz, T., & Botvin, E. (1995). Long term follow-up results of a randomized drug abuse prevention trial in a white middle class population. *Journal of the American Medical Association, 273,* 1106–1112.

Bowlby, J. (1969). *Attachment and loss: Vol. 1. Attachment.* New York: Basic Books.

Brazelton, T.B., & Greenspan, S.I. (2001). *The irreducible needs of children: What every child must have to grow, learn, and flourish.* Cambridge, MA: Perseus Publishing.

Bremner, J.D., & Narayan, M. (1998). The effects of stress on memory and the hippocampus throughout the life cycle: Implications for child development and aging. *Development and Psychopathology, 10,* 872–885.

Brendtro, L., & Larson, S. (2006). *The resilience revolution: Discovering strengths in challenging kids.* Bloomington, IN: Solution Tree.

Brendtro, L., Ness, A., & Mitchell, M. (2001). *No disposable kids.* Longmont, CO: Sopris West Educational Services.

Brooks, R. (1991). *The self-esteem teacher.* Circle Pines, MN: AGS Publishing.

Brown, C., & Thorpe, E. (1989). Individualizing training for early intervention practitioners. In E. Fenichel (Ed.), *Learning through supervision and mentorship to support the development of infants, toddlers and their families: A source book* (pp. 42–48). Washington, DC: ZERO TO THREE.

Bus, A.G., & van Ijzendoom, M.H. (1995). Mothers reading to their 3 year olds: The role of mother–child attachment security in becoming literate. *Reading Research Quarterly, 30*(4), 998–1015.

Cahill, L. (2000, January 19). *Emotions and memory.* Speech given at the Learning Brain Expo, San Diego.

California Attorney General's Office. (2002). *Safe from the start: Reducing children's exposure to violence.* Sacramento, CA: Crime and Violence Prevention Center.

Calkins, L.M. (2001). *The art of teaching reading.* New York: Longman

Clarke, G., Hawkins, W., Murphy, M., & Sheeber, L. (1993). School-based primary prevention of depressive symptomatology in adolescents: Findings from two studies. *Journal of Adolescent Research, 8,* 183–204.

Cohen, P., & Brook, J.S. (1995). The reciprocal influence of punishment and child behaviour disorder. In J. McCord (Ed.), *Coercion and punishment in long-term perspectives* (pp. 154–164). New York: Cambridge University Press.

Cole, S.F., O'Brien, J.G., Gadd, M.G., Ristuccia, J., Wallace, D.L., & Gregory, M. (2005). *Helping traumatized children learn: Supportive school environments for children traumatized by family violence.* Boston: Massachusetts Advocates for Children.

Connell, J.P., & Klem, A.M. (2000). You can get there from here: Using a theory of change approach to plan urban education reform. *Journal of Educational and Psychological Consultation, 11,* 93–120.

Cook, A., Spinazzola, J., Ford, J., Lanktree, C., Blaustein, M., Sprague, C., et al. (2007). Complex trauma in children and adolescents. *Focal Point, 21*(1), 4–8.

Cook, A., Spinazzola, J., Lanktree, C., Blaustein, M., Cloitre, M., DeRosa, R., et al. (2005). Complex trauma in children and adolescents. *Psychiatric Annals, 35,* 390–398.

Cooper, R.J. (2000). The impact of child abuse on children's play: A conceptual model. *Occupational Therapy International, 7,* 259–276.

Cozolino, L. (2002). *The neuroscience of psychotherapy: Building and rebuilding the human brain.* New York: W.W. Norton.

Cozolino, L. (2006). *The neuroscience of human relationships: Attachment and the developing social brain.* New York: W.W. Norton.

Craig, S.E. (1992). The educational needs of children living with violence. *Phi Delta Kappan, 74*(1), 67–71.

Craig, S.E. (2001, January 16). Remarks at Helping Traumatized Children Learn, a conference cosponsored by Lesley College, Massachusetts Advocates for Children (MAC), and the Task Force on Children Affected by Domestic Violence, Cambridge, MA. (Transcripts of the conference are on file at Massachusetts Advocates for Children, 25 Kingston Street, 2nd Floor, Boston, MA 02111; 617-357-8431)

Craig, S.E., Haggart, A.G., & Hull, K. (1999). Integrating therapies into the educational setting: Strategies for supporting children with severe disabilities. *Physical Disabilities, 17*(2), 91–109.

Dayton, T. (2000). *Trauma and addiction: Ending the cycle of pain through emotional literacy.* Deerfield Beach, FL: Health Communications.

Diamond, M., & Hopson, J. (1998). *Magic trees of the mind: How to nurture your child's intelligence, creativity, and healthy emotions from birth through adolescence.* New York: Dutton.

Dodge, K.A., Pettit, G.S., Bates, J.E., & Valente, E. (1995). Social information processing patterns partially mediate the effects of physical abuse on later conduct problems. *Journal of Abnormal Psychology, 104,* 632–643.

Doll, B., Sands, D.J., Wehmeyer, M.L., & Palmer, S. (1996). Promoting the development and acquisition of self-determined behavior. In D.J. Sands & M.L. Wehmeyer (Eds.), *Self-determination across the life span: Independence and choice for people with disabilities* (pp. 65–90). Baltimore: Paul H. Brookes Publishing Co.

Dyregrov, A. (2004). Educational consequences of loss and trauma. *Educational and Child Psychology, 21*(3), 77–84.

Elmore, R.F. (1996). Getting to scale with good educational practice. *Harvard Educational Review, 66*(1), 1–25.

Erikson, E. (1963). *Childhood and society.* New York: W.W. Norton.

Fantuzzo, J.W. (1991). Effects of interpersonal violence on psychological adjustment and competencies of young children. *Journal of Consulting and Clinical Psychology, 59,* 258–266.

Farragher, B., & Yanosy, S. (2005). Creating a trauma-sensitive culture in residential care. *The International Journal for Therapeutic and Supportive Organizations, 26*(1), 97–113.

Feerick, M.M., & Silverman, G.B. (Eds.). (2006). *Children exposed to violence.* Baltimore: Paul H. Brookes Publishing Co.

Feldman, R., Salzinger, S., Rosario, M., & Alvardo, L. (1995). Parent, teacher and peer ratings of physically abused and non maltreated children's behavior. *Journal of Abnormal Child Psychology, 23*(3), 317–334.

Felitti, V.J., Anda, R.F., Nordenberg, D., Williamson, D.F., Spitz, A.M., Edwards, V., et al. (1998). Relationship of childhood abuse and household dysfunction to many of the leading causes of death in adults. *American Journal of Preventive Medicine, 14,* 245–258.

Feuertein, R. (1980). *Instrumental enrichment: An intervention program for cognitive modifiability.* Baltimore: University Park Press.

Figley, C.R. (1995). *Treating compassion fatigue: Coping with secondary traumatic stress disorder in those who treat the traumatized.* New York: Brunner/Mazel.

Figley, C.R. (2003) *Compassion fatigue: An introduction.* Retrieved October 20, 2006, from http://www.greencross.org/_Research/CompassionFatigue.asp

Fonagy, P., Steele, M., Steele, H., Higgitt, A., & Target, M. (1994). The theory and practice of resilience. *Journal of Child Psychology and Psychiatry, 35,* 231–257.

Fonagy, P., & Target, M. (1998). Mentalization and the changing aims of child psychoanalysis. *Psychoanalytic Dialogues, 8,* 87–114.

Fosha, D. (2000). *The transforming power of affect: A model of accelerated change.* New York: Basic Books.

Fosha, D. (2003). Dyadic regulation and experiential work with emotion and relatedness in trauma and disorganized attachment. In M.F. Solomon & D.J. Siegel (Eds.), *Healing trauma: Attachment, mind, body, and brain* (pp. 221–281). New York: W.W. Norton.

Fredericks, L. (1997). *Developing skills literacy through storytelling.* Retrieved January 1, 2007, from http://www.nationalserviceresources.org/resources/newsletters/resource_connection/volume_2_number_4/developing_literacy.php

Frey, N., & Fisher, D. (2004). The role of the literacy professional in addressing the disproportionate representation of culturally and linguistically diverse students in special education, In D. Lapp, C.C. Block, E.J. Cooper, J. Flood, N. Roser, & J.V. Tinajero (Eds.), *Teaching all the children: Strategies for developing literacy in an urban setting* (pp. 231–255). New York: Guilford Press.

Friend, M. (1996). *The power of two: Making a difference through co-teaching* [Videotape]. Bloomington, IN: A Forum on Education, Indiana University Television Services, and Elephant Rock Productions.

Frosch, C.A., Cox, M.J., & Goldman, B.D. (2001). Infant–parent attachment and parental child behavior during parent toddler storybook interactions. *Merrill-Palmer Quarterly, 47*(4), 445–474.

Garbarino, J., Dubrow, N., Kostelny, K., & Pardo, C. (1992). *Children in danger: Coping with the consequences of community violence.* San Francisco: Jossey-Bass.

Gazzaniga, M. (1998). *The mind's past.* Berkeley: University of California Press.

Giangreco, M.F. (1994). Effects of a consensus building process on team decision making: Preliminary data. *Physical Disabilities: Education and Related Services, 13*(1), 41–58.

Goleman, D. (1995). *Emotional intelligence: Why it matters more than IQ.* New York: Bantum Books.

Greenburg, M., Kusche, C., Cook, E., & Quamma, J. (1995). Promoting emotional competence in school aged children: The effects of the PATHS curriculum. *Development and Psychopathology, 7,* 117–136.

Greene, R. (2001). *The explosive child: A new approach for understanding and parenting easily frustrated, chronically inflexible children.* New York: HarperCollins.

Greene, R., & Ablon, S. (2006). *Treating explosive kids: The collaborative problem-solving approach.* New York: Guilford Press.

Greenspan, S.I. (1997). *The growth of the mind and the endangered nature of intelligence.* Reading, MA: Perseus.

Gregg, S. (1998). School-based programs to promote safety and civility. *AEL Policy Briefs.* Charleston, WV: Appalachia Educational Laboratory.

Groves, B.M. (2002). *Children who see too much.* Boston: Beacon Press.

Han, S., & Weiss, B. (2005). Sustainability of teacher implementation of school-based mental health programs. *Journal of Abnormal Child Psychology, 33*(6), 665–679.

Haeseler, L.A. (2006). Promoting literacy learning for children of abuse: Strategies for elementary school teachers. *Reading Improvement, 43*(3), 136–142.

Hart, L. (1998). *Human brain and human learning* (updated). Black Diamond, WA: Books for Educators.

Harvey, M.R. (1996). An ecological view of psychological trauma and trauma recovery. *Journal of Traumatic Stress, 9*(1), 3–23.

Hawkins, J.D., Catalano, R.E., Kosterman, R., Abbott, R., & Hill, K. (1999). Preventing adolescent health risk behaviors by strengthening protection during childhood. *Archives of Pediatric and Adolescent Medicine, 153,* 226–234.

Hawkins. J.D., Guo, J., Hill, K.G., Battin-Pearson, S., & Abbott, R.D. (1996). Long-term effects of the Seattle Social Development Intervention on school bonding trajectories. *Applied Developmental Science, 5*(4), 225–236.

Helfer, R.E., & Kempe, C.H. (1980). Developmental deficits which limit interpersonal skills. In R.E. Helfer & C.H. Kempe (Eds.), *The battered child* (3rd ed., pp. 36–48). Chicago: University of Chicago Press.

Henry, J., Sloane, M., & Black-Pond, C. (2007). Neurobiology and Neurodevelopmental impact of childhood traumatic stress and pre-natal alcohol abuse. *Language, Speech and Hearing Services in Schools, 38,* 99–108.

Herman, J.L. (1992). *Trauma and recovery.* New York: Basic Books.

Horsman, J. (2000). *Too scared to learn: Women, violence, and education.* Mahwah, NJ: Lawrence Erlbaum Associates.

Howard, A.C. (1986). Developmental play stages of physically abused and non-abused children. *The American Journal of Occupational Therapy, 40,* 691–695.

Hyter, Y., Henry, J., Atchison, B., Sloane, M., Black-Pond, C., & Shangraw, K. (2003). Children affected by trauma and alcohol exposure: A profile of the Southwestern Michigan Children's Trauma Assessment Center. *The ASHA Leader, 8*(21), 6–7, 14.

Jackson, H. (2004). *Helping students cope with trauma and loss: Online training for school personnel* [Online course]. Retrieved November 25, 2007, from http://ci.columbia.edu/w0521

Jackson, S.E., Schwab, R.L., & Schuler, R.S. (1986). Toward an understanding of the burnout phenomenon. *Journal of Applied Psychology, 71,* 630–640.

Jensen, E. (1998a). How Julie's brain learns. *Educational Leadership, 56*(3), 41–45.

Jensen, E. (1998b). *Teaching with the brain in mind.* Alexandria, VA: Association for Supervision and Curriculum Development.

Jensen, P. (2002). *Report on Emotional and Behavioral Disorders in Youth, 2*(4), 82–86.

Jensen, P., & Cooper, J. (2002). *Attention deficit hyperactivity disorder: State of science, best practices.* Kingston, NJ: Civic Research Institute.

Johnson, D., & Johnson, R. (1985). *Cooperative learning: Warm ups, grouping strategies and group activities.* Edina, MN: Interaction Book Company.

Johnson, J. (2007). *Finding your smile again.* St. Paul, MN: Redleaf Press.

Jonson-Reid, M. (2004). A prospective analysis of the relationship between reported maltreatment and special education eligibility among poor children. *Child Maltreatment, 9*(4), 382–394.

Katz, M. (1997). *On playing a poor hand well: Insights from the lives of those who have overcome childhood risks and adversities.* New York: W.W. Norton.

Koplow, L. (1996). *Unsmiling faces*. New York: Teachers College Press.

Kotulak, R. (1996). *Inside the brain: Revolutionary discoveries of how the mind works*. Kansas City, MO: Andrews & McMeel.

Lamude, K.G., Scudder, J., & Furno-Lamude, D. (1992). The relationship of student resistance strategies in the classroom to teacher burnout and teacher type A behavior. *Journal of Social Behavior and Personality, 7*, 597–610.

LaVoie, R. (1994). *Last one picked . . . first one picked on* [Videotape]. Washington, DC: WETA-TV.

LaVoie, R. (2005). *It's so much work to be your friend: Helping the child with learning disabilities find social success*. New York: Simon & Schuster.

LeDoux, J. (2002). *Synaptic self: How our brains become who we are*. New York: Penguin Books.

Levine, M. (2002a). *A mind at a time*. New York: Simon & Schuster.

Levine, M. (2002b). *All kinds of minds: A young student's book about learning abilities and learning disorders*. New York: Simon & Schuster.

Levine, P., & Kline, M. (2007). *Trauma through a child's eyes: Awakening the ordinary miracle of healing*. Berkeley, CA: North Atlantic Books.

Lewis, M. (2003). The role of the self in shame. *Social Research, 70*(4), 1181–1204.

Lieberman, A. (2007, May 7). Remarks at Child Witness to Violence 10th Anniversary conference, Boston.

Liston, D., Whitcomb, J., & Borko, H. (2006). Too little or too much: Teacher preparation and the first years of teaching. *The Journal of Teacher Education, 57*(4), 351–359.

Long, N. (1998). *The conflict cycle paradigm* [Videotape]. Allentown, PA: Pennsylvania Community Learning and Information Network and KidsPeace Creative Services.

Long, N., & Dufner, B. (1980). The stress cycle or the coping cycle: The impact of home and school stresses on pupil's classroom behavior. In N. Long, W.C. Morse, & R.G. Neuman (Eds.), *Conflict in the classroom* (4th ed., pp. 218–228). Belmont, CA: Wadsworth Publishing Company.

Lubit, R., Rovine, D., Defrancisci, L., & Eth, S. (2003). Impact of trauma on children. *Journal of Psychiatric Practice, 9*(2), 128–138, 133.

Lyons-Ruth, K., Connell, D., Zoll, D., & Stahl, J. (1987). Infants at social risk: relations among infant maltreatment, maternal behavior, and infant attachment behavior. *Developmental Psychology, 23*, 223–232.

Main, M., & Solomon, M. (1990). Procedures for identifying infants as disorganized/disoriented during the Ainsworth Strange Situation. In M.T. Greenberg, D. Cicchetti, & E.M. Cummings (Eds.), *Attachment in the pre-school years* (pp. 121–160). Chicago: University of Chicago Press.

Margolin, G., & Gordis, E.B. (2000). The effects of family and community violence on children. *Annual Review of Psychology, 51*, 445–479.

Martin, S.E., & Clements, M.L. (2002). Young children's responding to inter-parental conflict: Associations with marital aggression and child adjustment. *Journal of Child and Family Studies, 11*(2), 231–244.

Marzano, R.J., Pickering, D.J., & Pollack, J.E. (2001). *Classroom instruction that works: Research-based strategies for increasing student achievement.* Alexandria, VA: Association for Supervision and Curriculum Development.

Masten, A.S., & Coatsworth, J.D. (1995). Competence, resilience, and psychopathology. In D. Cicchetti & D.J. Cohen (Eds.), *Developmental psychology: Vol. 2. Risk, disorder, and adaptation* (pp. 715–752). New York: Wiley.

McLaughlin, M.W., & Mitra, D. (2001). Theory based change and change based theory: Going deeper, going broader. *Journal of Educational Change, 2,* 301–332.

Miller, A. (1984). *Thou shalt not be aware.* New York: Farrar, Straus, Giroux.

Morris, P.E., & Cook, N. (1978). When do first letter mnemonics aid recall? *British Journal of Educational Psychology, 48,* 22–28.

Morrow, G. (1987). *The compassionate school: A practical guide to educating abused and traumatized children.* Upper Saddle River, NJ: Prentice Hall.

National Child Traumatic Stress Network. (2003). *General statistics on prevalence, correlates, and consequences of child trauma* [PowerPoint presentation]. Retrieved November 27, 2007, from www.nctsnet.org/nctsn_assets/ppt/powerpoints/general_statistics.ppt

Niehoff, D. (1999). *Biology of violence.* New York: Simon & Schuster.

O'Connell-Higgins, G. (1994). *Resilient adults: Overcoming a cruel past.* San Francisco: Jossey-Bass.

Oden, S. (1988). Alternative perspectives on children's peer relationships. In. T.D. Yawkey & J.E. Johnson (Eds.), *Integrative processes and socialization: Early to middle childhood* (pp. 139–161). Mahwah, NJ: Lawrence Erlbaum Associates.

Osofsky, J.D. (1999). The impact of violence on children. *Domestic Violence and Children, 9*(3), 33–49.

Osofsky, J.D., & Fenichel, E. (1994). *Caring for infants and toddlers in violent environments: Hurt, healing, hope.* Washington, DC: ZERO TO THREE.

Osofsky, J.D., & Osofsky, H.J. (1999). Developmental implications of violence in youth. In M. Levine, W.B. Carey, & A.C. Crocker (Eds.), *Developmental and behavioral pediatrics* (3rd ed., pp. 493–498). Philadelphia: W.B. Saunders.

Palinscar, A.S., & Brown, A.C. (1984). Reciprocal teaching of comprehension: Fostering and monitoring activities. *Cognition and Instruction, 1,* 117–175.

Payne, R. (1996). *A framework for understanding poverty.* Highlands, TX: aha! Process.

Perry, B.D. (1994). Neurobiological sequelae of childhood trauma: Post traumatic stress disorders in children. In M. Murberg (Ed.), *Catecholamines in post traumatic stress disorder: Emerging concepts* (pp. 253–276). Washington, DC: American Psychiatric Press.

Perry, B.D. (2002). Neurodevelopmental impact of violence in childhood. In D.H. Schetky & E.P. Benedek (Eds.), *Principles and practice of child and adolescent forensic psychiatry* (pp. 191–203). Washington, DC: American Psychiatric Publishing.

Perry, B.D. (2006). Applying principles of neurodevelopment to clinical work with maltreated and traumatized children: The neurosequential model of therapeutics. In N.B. Webb (Ed.), *Working with traumatized youth in child welfare* (pp. 27–52). New York: Guilford Press.

Perry, B.D. & Pollard, R. (1998). Homeostasis, stress, trauma, and adaptation: A neurodevelopmental view of childhood trauma. *Child and Adolescent Psychiatric Clinics of North America, 7*(1), 33–51.

Petit, M., & Brooks, T.R. (1998). Abuse and delinquency: Two sides of the same coin. *Reclaiming Children and Youth, 7*(2), 77–79.

Piaget, J. (1932). *Language and thought of the child.* London: Kegan, Paul, Trench, Trubner, and Co.

Pollack, S., Klorman, R., Thatcher, J.E., & Cicchetti, D. (2001). P3b reflects maltreated children's reactions to facial displays of emotion. *Psychophysiology, 38,* 267–74.

Pollack, S., & Tolley-Schell, S. (2003). Selective attention to facial emotion in physically abused children. *Journal of Abnormal Psychology 112,* 323–338.

Pressley, M. (2000). What should comprehension instruction be the construction of? In M.L. Kamil, P.B. Mosenthal, P.D. Pearson, & R. Barr (Eds.) *Handbook of reading research* (pp. 545–563). Mahwah, NJ: Lawrence Erlbaum Associates.

Pynoos, R.S., Steinberg, A.M., & Goenjian, A. (1996). Traumatic stress in childhood and adolescence: Recent developments and current controversies. In B.A. van der Kolk, A. MacFarlane. & L. Weisaeth (Eds.), *Traumatic stress: The effects of overwhelming experience on the mind, body and society* (pp. 331–358). New York: Guilford Press.

Quarantelli, E.L., & Dynes, R. (1977). Response to social crisis and disaster. *Annual Review of Sociology, 2,* 23–49.

RAND Reading Study Group. (2002). *Reading for understanding: Toward an R&D program for reading comprehension.* Santa Monica, CA: RAND.

Raphael, T.E., & McMahon, S.I. (1994). Book club: An alternative structure for reading instruction. *Reading Teacher, 48,* 102–116.

Ratey, J. (2001). *A user's guide to the brain: Perception, attention, and the four theatres of the brain.* New York: Vintage Books.

Raver, C.C. (2004). Placing emotional self-regulation in sociocultural and socioeconomic contexts. *Child Development, 75*(2), 346–353.

Ringeisen, H., Henderson, K., & Hoagwood, K. (2003). Context matters: Schools and the "research to practice gap" in children's mental health. *School Psychology Review, 32*(2), 153–161.

Roans, M., & Hoagwood, K. (2000). School based mental health services: A research review. *Clinical Child and Family Psychology Review, 3,* 223–241.

Rogers-Adkinson, D.L., & Hooper, S.R. (2003). The relationship of language and behavior: Introduction to special issue. *Behavior Disorders, 29*(1), 12–20.

Rutherford, R. (2002). *Instruction for all students.* Alexandria, VA: Just ASK Publications.

Sanford, L. (1990). *Strong at the broken places: Overcoming the trauma of child abuse.* New York: Avon Books.

Scaer, R. (2005). *The trauma spectrum: Hidden wounds and human resiliency.* New York: W.W. Norton.

Schacter, D.L. (2001). *The seven sins of memory: How the mind forgets and remembers.* New York: Houghton Mifflin.

Schore, A.N. (1994). *Affect regulation and the origin of the self: The neurobiology of emotional development.* Mahwah, NJ: Lawrence Erlbaum Associates.

Schore, A.N. (2000). Attachment and the regulation of the right brain. *Attachment and Human Development, 2*(1), 23–47.

Schore, A.N. (2001). The effects of early relational trauma on right brain development, affect regulation, and infant mental health. *Infant Mental Health Journal, 22,* 201–269.

Schunk, D.H., & Rice, J.M. (1993). Strategy fading and progress feedback: Effects on self-efficacy and comprehension among students receiving remedial reading services. *Journal of Special Education, 27*(3), 257–276.

Sears, R.R., Maccoby, E.E., & Lewin, H. (1957). *Patterns of child rearing.* New York: Harper Row.

Seligman, M., Reivich, K., Joycox, L., & Gillham, J. (1995). *The optimistic child: A proven program to safeguard children against depression and build lifelong resilience.* New York: HarperCollins.

Shanok, R.S. (1989). The supervisory relationship: Integrator, resource and guide. In E. Fenichel (Ed.), *Learning through supervision and mentorship to support the development of infants, toddlers, and their families: A source book* (pp. 37–41). Washington, DC: ZERO TO THREE.

Shields, A., & Cicchetti, D. (2001). Parental maltreatment and emotional dysregulation as risk factors for bullying and victimization in middle childhood. *Journal of Clinical and Child Psychology, 30,* 349–363.

Shonk, S.M., & Ciccheti, D. (2001). Maltreatment, competency deficits, and risk for academic and behavioral maladjustment. *Developmental Psychology, 37*(1), 3–17.

Shores, R.E., & Wehby, J.H. (1999). Analyzing social behavior of children with emotional and behavioral disorders in classrooms. *Journal of Emotional and Behavioral Disorders, 7,* 194–199.

Siegel, D.J. (1999). *The developing mind: Toward a neurobiology of interpersonal experience.* New York: Guilford Press.

Siegel, D.J. (2007). *The mindful brain: Reflection and attunement in the cultivation of well-being.* New York: W.W. Norton.

Solomon, M.F. (2003). Connection, disruption, repair: Treating the effects of attachment trauma on intimate relationships. In M.F. Solomon & D.J. Siegel (Eds.), *Healing trauma: Attachment, mind, body, and brain* (pp. 322–345). New York: W.W. Norton.

Solomon, M.F., & Siegel, D.J. (Eds.). (2003). *Healing trauma: Attachment, mind, body, and brain.* New York: W.W. Norton.

Spinazzola, J., Blaustein, M., & van der Kolk, B.A. (2005). Posttraumatic stress disorder treatment outcome research: The study of unrepresentative samples? *Journal of Traumatic Stress, 18*(5), 425–436.

Sprenger, M. (1999). *Becoming a "wiz" at brain-based teaching: How to make every year your best school year.* Thousand Oaks, CA: Corwin Press.

Squire, L.R. & Zola-Morgan, S. (1991). The medial temporal lobe memory system. *Science, 253,* 1380–1386.

Stein, P., & Kendall, J. (2004). *Psychological trauma and the developing brain: Neurologically based interventions for troubled children.* New York: The Haworth Press.

Steiner, H., Zeanah, C.H., Studer, M., Ash, P., & Angell, R. (1994). The hidden faces of trauma: An update on child psychiatric traumatology. *Scientific Proceedings of the Annual Meeting of the American Academy of Child and Adolescent Psychiatry, 3,* 1.

Straus, M. (2006). *The primordial violence: Corporal punishment by parents, cognitive development, and crime.* Walnut Creek CA: Alta Mira.

Straus, M.A., & Stewart, J. (1999). Corporal punishment by American parents: National data on prevalence, chronicity, severity, and duration, in relation to child, and family characteristics. *Clinical Child and Family Psychology Review, 2,* 55–70.

Streeck-Fischer, A., & van der Kolk, B.A. (2000). Down will come baby, cradle and all: Diagnostic and therapeutic implications of chronic trauma on child development. *Australian and New Zealand Journal of Psychiatry, 34,* 903–918.

Sugai, G., Horner, R.H., Dunlap, G., Hieneman, M., Lewis, T., Nelson, C., et al. (2000). Applying positive behavior support and functional behavior assessment in the schools. *Journal of Positive Behavior Interventions, 2*(3), 131–143.

Swanson, H.L. (1988). Memory subtypes in learning disabled readers. *Learning Disabilities Quarterly, 11,* 342–357.

Sylwester, R. (1995). *A celebration of neurons: An educator's guide to the human brain.* Alexandria, VA: Association for Supervision and Curriculum Development.

Sylwester, R. (1999). In search of the roots of adolescent aggression. *Educational Leadership, 57*(1), 65–69.

Teicher, M. (2002). Scars that won't heal: The neurobiology of child abuse. *Scientific American, 286*(3), 68–75.

Teicher, M.H., Anderson, S.L., Polcari, A., Anderson, C.M., & Navalta, C.P. (2002). Developmental neurobiology of childhood stress and trauma. *Psychiatric Clinics of North America, 25,* 397–426.

Thomas, A., Chess, S., Birch, H.G., Herzig, M.E., & Korn, S. (1963). *Behavioral individuality in early childhood.* New York: New York University Press.

Tomlinson, C.A. (2001). *How to differentiate instruction in mixed ability classrooms* (2nd ed.). Alexandria, VA: Association for Supervision and Curriculum Development.

Tomlinson, C.A., & Eidson, C.C. (2003). *Differentiation in practice: A resource guide for differentiating curriculum, grades K–5.* Alexandria, VA: Association for Supervision and Curriculum Development.

Tovani, C. (2000). *I read it, but I don't get it: Comprehension strategies for adolescent readers.* Portland, ME: Stenhouse.

Turnbull, A., Edmonson, H., Griggs, P., Wickham, D., Sailor, W., Freeman, R., et al. (2002). A blueprint for school wide positive behavior support: Implementation of three components. *Exceptional Children, 68,* 377–402.

United Nations Children's Fund & The Bodyshop International. (2006). *Behind closed doors: The impact of domestic violence on children* [Brochure]. Retrieved November 27, 2007, from http://www.unicef.org/media/files/BehindClosed Doors.pdf

van der Kolk, B.A. (2001, January 16). Remarks at Helping Traumatized Children Learn, a conference cosponsored by Lesley College, Massachusetts Advocates for Children (MAC), and the Task Force on Children Affected by Domestic Violence, Cambridge, MA. (Transcripts of the conference are on file at Massachusetts Advocates for Children, 25 Kingston Street, 2nd Floor, Boston, MA 02111; 617-357-8431)

van der Kolk, B.A. (2005). Developmental trauma disorder. *Psychiatric Annals, 35*(5), 401–408.

van der Kolk, B.A., & McFarlane, A. (1996). The black hole of trauma. In B.A. van der Kolk, A. McFarlane, & L. Weisaeth (Eds.), *Traumatic stress: The effects of overwhelming experience on mind, body and society* (pp. 3–23). New York: Guilford Press.

Vygotsky, L.S. (1986). The genetic roots of thought and speech. In A. Kozulin (Ed. & Trans.). *Thoughts and language* (Rev. ed.) Cambridge, MA: MIT Press.

Watson, S.M.R., & Westby, C.E. (2003). Prenatal drug exposure: Implications for personnel preparation. *Remedial and Special Education, 24*(4), 204–214.

Weist, M.D., Lowie, J.A., Flaherty, L.T., & Pruitt, D. (2001). Collaboration among the education, mental health, and public health systems to promote young mental health. *Psychiatric Services, 52,* 1348–1351.

Westling, D., Herzog, M.J., Cooper-Duffy, K., Prohn, K., & Ray, M. (2006). The teacher support program: A proposed resource for the special education profession and an initial validation. *Remedial and Special Education, 27*(3), 136–147.

Widom, C.S. (2000, January). Childhood victimization: Early adversity and later psychopathology. *National Institute of Justice Journal, 242.* Retrieved November 27, 2007, from http://www.ncjrs.gov/pdffiles1/jr000242b.pdf

Wolfe, P. (2001). *Brain matters: Translating research into classroom practice.* Alexandria, VA: Association for Supervision and Curriculum Development.

Wolinsky, S. (1991). *Trances people live: Healing approaches to quantum psychology.* Falls Village, CT: The Bramble Co.

Wooten, D., & Cullinan, B. (2004) Metacognition through writing and sharing connections. In D. Lapp, C.C. Block, E.J. Cooper, J. Flood, N. Roser & J.V. Tinajero (Eds.), *Teaching all the children: Strategies for developing literacy in an urban setting* (pp. 294–305). New York: Guilford Press.

York, J., Rainforth, B., & Giangreco, M.F. (1990). Transdisciplinary teamwork and integrated therapy: Clarifying some misconceptions. *Pediatric Physical Therapy, 2*(2), 73–79.

Resources

Suggested Books for Students

Bang, M. (1999). *When Sophie gets angry—really, really angry.* New York: Blue Sky Press. (Ages 4–8)

Buffie, M. (2006). *Out of focus.* Toronto: Kids Can Press. (Ages 9–12)

Cain, J. (2000). *The way I feel.* Seattle: Parenting Press. (Ages 4–8)

Campbell, B.M., & Lewis, E.B. (2003). *Sometimes my mommy gets angry.* New York: G.P. Putnam's Sons. (Ages 4–8)

Crist, J.J. (2004). *What to do when you're scared and worried: A guide for kids.* Minneapolis, MN: Free Spirit. (Ages 9–12)

Curtis, J.L., & Cornell, L. (1998). *Today I feel silly and other moods that make my day.* New York: HarperCollins. (Ages 4–8)

Curtis, J.L., & Cornell, L. (2004). *It's hard to be five: Learning how to work my control panel.* New York: Joanna Cotler Books. (Ages 4–8)

Deaton, W., & Johnson, K. (1991). *Living with my family.* Claremont, CA: Hunter House. (Ages 9–12)

Deaton, W., & Johnson, K. (2002). *I saw it happen: A child's workbook about witnessing violence.* Claremont, CA: Hunter House. (Ages 4–8)

Deaton, W., & Johnson, K. (2002). *My own thoughts and feelings on stopping the hurt: A child's workbook about exploring hurt and abuse.* Claremont, CA: Hunter House. (Ages 4–8)

Deaton, W., & Johnson, K. (2002). *No more hurt: A child's workbook about recovering from abuse.* Claremont, CA: Hunter House. (Ages 9–12)

Desetta, A., & Wolin, S. (2000). *The struggle to be strong: True stories by teens about overcoming tough times.* Minneapolis, MN: Free Spirit. (Ages 11 and older)

Fitzgerald, H. (2000). *The grieving teen: A guide for teenagers and their friends.* New York: Simon & Schuster. (Ages 11 and older)

Goldblatt, R. (2004). *The boy who didn't want to be sad.* Washington, DC: Magination Press. (Ages 4–8)

Gootman, M.E., & Espeland, P. (2005). *When a friend dies: A book for teens about grieving and healing* (Rev. and updated ed.). Minneapolis: Free Spirit. (Ages 11 and older)

Harris, R.H., & Ormerod, J. (2001). *Goodbye, Mousie.* New York: Margaret K. McElderry Books. (Ages 4–8)

Hipp, E., Espeland, P., & Fleishman, M. (1995). *Fighting invisible tigers: A stress management guide for teens.* Minneapolis, MN: Free Spirit. (Ages 11 and older)

Hipp, E., & Hanson, L.K. (1995). *Help for the hard times: Getting through loss.* Center City, MN: Hazelden. (Ages 11 and older)

Holmes, M.M., Mudlaff, S.J., & Pillo, C. (2000). *A terrible thing happened.* Washington, DC: Magination Press. (Ages 4–8)

Jackson, E.B., & Rotner, S. (2002). *Sometimes bad things happen.* Brookfield, CT: Millbrook Press. (Ages 4–8)

Lehman, C. (2005). *Strong at the heart: How it feels to heal from sexual abuse.* New York: Farrar, Straus and Giroux. (Ages 14 and older)

Loftis, C., & Gallagher, C. (1995). *The words hurt.* Far Hills, NJ: New Horizon Press. (Ages 4–8)

Mather, C.L., & Debye, K.E. (2004). *How long does it hurt? A guide to recovering from incest and sexual abuse for teenagers, their friends, and their families.* San Francisco: Jossey-Bass. (Ages 11 and older)

Moser, A., & Melton, D. (1994). *Don't rant and rave on Wednesdays! The children's anger-control book.* Kansas City, MO: Landmark Editions. (Ages 4–8)

Mundy, M., & Alley, R.W. (1998). *Sad isn't bad: A good-grief guidebook for kids dealing with loss.* St. Meinrad, IN: One Caring Place. (Ages 9–12)

Pledge, D.S. (2003). *When something feels wrong: A survival guide about abuse for young people.* Minneapolis, MN: Free Spirit. (Ages 14 and older)

Ritter, J.H. (2000). *Over the wall.* New York: Philomel Books. (Ages 11–13)

Romain, T., & Verdick, E. (1999). *What on earth do you do when someone dies?* Minneapolis, MN: Free Spirit. (Ages 9–12)

Schor, H., & Kilpatrick, M. (2002). *A place for Starr: A story of hope for children experiencing family violence.* Indianapolis, IN: Kidsrights. (Ages 9–12)

Schwiebert, P., DeKlyen, C., & Bills, T. (2001). *Tear soup: A recipe for healing after loss* (2nd ed.). Portland, OR: Grief Watch. (Ages 4–8)

Seaward, B.L., & Bartlett, L. (2002). *Hot stones and funny bones: Teens helping teens cope with stress and anger.* Deerfield Beach, FL: Health Communications. (Ages 11 and older)

Shuman, C., & Pillo, C. (2003). *Jenny is scared: When sad things happen in the world.* Washington, DC: Magination Press. (Ages 4–8)

Silverman, J.L. (1999). *Help me say goodbye: Activities for helping kids cope when a special person dies.* Minneapolis, MN: Fairview Press. (Ages 4–8)

Spelman, C., & Parkinson, K. (2002). *When I feel scared.* Morton Grove, IL: Albert Whitman & Co. (Ages 2–8)

Thomas, P., & Harker, L. (2001). *I miss you: A first look at death.* Hauppauge, NY: Barron's Educational Series. (Ages 4–8)

Trottier, M., & Friedman, J. (1997). *A safe place.* Morton Grove, IL: A. Whitman. (Ages 3–8)

Verdick, E., & Lisovskis, M. (2003). *How to take the grrrr out of anger.* Minneapolis, MN: Free Spirit. (Ages 9–12)

Vincent, E. (2007). *Grief girl: My true story.* New York: Delacorte Press. (Ages 14 and older)

Wood, J.R. (1995). *When pigs fly.* New York: G.P. Putnam's Sons. (Ages 9–12)

Wood, J.R. (1997). *Turtle on a fence post.* New York: G.P. Putnam's Sons. (Ages 9–12)

Wolfelt, A.D. (2001). *Healing your grieving heart for teens: 100 practical ideas.* Fort Collins, CO: Companion Press. (Ages 12 and older)

Wolfelt, A.D. (2002). *The healing your grieving heart journal for teens.* Fort Collins, CO: Companion Press. (Ages 12 and older)

Index